TEACHER'S PET PUBLICATIONS

LITPLAN TEACHER PACK
for
Oedipus Rex
based on the play by
Sophocles

Translation by
Dudley Fitts & Robert Fitzgerald

Written by
Susan R. Woodward

© 2007 Teacher's Pet Publications
All Rights Reserved

This **LitPlan** for *Oedipus Rex*

has been brought to you by Teacher's Pet Publications, Inc.

Copyright Teacher's Pet Publications 2007

Only the student materials in this unit plan (such as worksheets, study questions, and tests) may be reproduced multiple times for use in the purchaser's classroom.

For any additional copyright questions,
contact Teacher's Pet Publications.

www.tpet.com

TABLE OF CONTENTS
Oedipus Rex

Introduction	6
Unit Objectives	8
Reading Assignment Sheet	9
Unit Outline	10
Study Questions (Short Answer)	13
Answer Key (Short Answer)	15
Quiz/Study Questions (Multiple Choice)	21
Answer Key (Multiple Choice)	33
Pre-reading Vocabulary Worksheets	37
Answer Key (Vocabulary Worksheets)	49
Lesson One (Introductory Lesson)	53
Nonfiction Assignment Sheet	58
Oral Reading Evaluation Form	60
Peer Review Form: Performance	61
Writing Assignment 1: Aristotle's Poetics	68
Writing Evaluation Form	69
Writing Assignment 2: Composing Odes	73
Vocabulary Review Activities	75
Extra Writing Assignments/Discussion ?s	78
Writing Assignment 3: Who's At Fault?	81
Peer Editing Form: Persuasive Writing	83
Presentation Evaluation Sheet	86
Peer Critique Form	87
Unit Review Activities	88
Unit Tests	93
Unit Resource Materials	133
Vocabulary Resource Materials	154

A FEW NOTES ABOUT THE AUTHOR: SOPHOCLES

Sophocles was born in Colonus, a small town outside of Athens, Greece in 495 B.C. He was the son of an armor manufacturer who became schooled in poetry, music, and dancing. He was prized for his exceptional physique and abilities in the arts. When he was fifteen years old, Sophocles earned his reputation as a performer when he was selected to lead a chorus of boys in the paean (a hymn of victory and thanksgiving to the gods) after the battle of Salamis. He went on to become an established playwright in Athens, authoring more than 120 plays.

Sophocles first public recognition as a playwright came when he won first prize at the festival of Dionysus (called the *Dionysia*) in 468 B.C. At these festivals, playwrights were to complete three tragedies and one satyr-play (collectively, this was called a *tetralogy;* "tetra" means "four"). This particular festival's outcome was significant for his career because the twenty-eight year old Sophocles won the coveted prize over Athens' established playwright, Aeschylus. As the years continued, Sophocles went on to win first prize a total of twenty-four times (since each tetralogy consisted of four plays, he wrote ninety-six first place award winning plays), and seven second place awards out of the thirty-one competitions he entered. Sadly, out of over one hundred twenty plays written by Sophocles, only seven still exist in their entirety. These are:

Ajax	445 B.C.
Antigone	440 B.C.
Electra	440 B.C.
Oedipus Rex	430 B.C.
The Trachiniae	413 B.C.
Philoctetes	410 B.C.
Odeipus at Colonus	401 B.C. (date of first performance; five years after the death of Sophocles)

Although the Oedipus plays (*Oedipus Rex, Oedipus at Colonus,* and *Antigone)* are commonly thought of as a trilogy, they were not written as such (see above dates). Also, since there are inconsistencies in characterizations and events between them, the plays are best studied an individual works rather than part of a trilogy.

Sophocles was also involved in the technical aspect of the Greek theatre as well. He introduced the idea of painted scenery, variations in the types of music sung by the chorus, as well as increasing the size of the cast: the chorus went from twelve members to fifteen, and the number of actors in a production increased from two to three. The elaborate costumes (especially the masks) allowed the actors to portray numerous characters throughout the production. With the addition of a third actor on the stage, plot development and distinguishing between characters became more comprehensive to the audiences.

Although most of Sophocles' life centered on theatre and writing (he also wrote poetry), he was also involved at a civic level. He served as a general under Pericles in the army and was a key negotiator in the Peloponnesian War. In his role as a priest, Sophocles was concerned with the individual's need to find his/her own place in the moral and cosmic order of the universe. His plays contain moral lessons that usually pertain to man's duty to the gods and the avoidance of excessive pride. Late in life, Sophocles acted as a statesman who helped organize the recovery of Athens after it was defeated at Syracuse.

Sophocles was said to have been especially blessed by the gods, and he was highly revered in his society. His physical beauty, strength, sense of fairness, and talent earned him the admiration of those around him, and upon his death in 406 B.C., Athens mourned. A shrine, called *Dexion* (The Entertainer) was established in his honor, and annual sacrifices were offered in his memory.

INTRODUCTION

This LitPlan has been designed to develop students' reading, writing, thinking, and language skills through exercises and activities related to *Oedipus Rex*. It includes 19 lessons, supported by extra resource materials.

The **introductory lesson** introduces students to Greek Theatre and the Oedipus Myth involving the Riddle of the Sphinx. This mythological tale actually takes place years before the plague that Thebes is suffering at the opening of *Oedipus Rex*. Following the introductory activity, students are given a transition to explain how the activity relates to the play they are about to read. Following the transition, students are given the materials they will be using during the unit. At the end of the lesson, students begin the pre-reading work for the first reading assignment.

The **reading assignments** are approximately fifteen to twenty pages each; some are a little shorter while others are a little longer. Students have approximately 15 minutes of pre-reading work to do prior to each reading assignment. This pre-reading work involves reviewing the study questions for the assignment and doing some vocabulary work for 10 vocabulary words they will encounter in their reading.

The **study guide questions** are fact-based questions; students can find the answers to these questions right in the text. These questions come in two formats: short answer or multiple choice. The best use of these materials is probably to use the short answer version of the questions as study guides for students (since answers will be more complete), and to use the multiple choice version for occasional quizzes.

The **vocabulary work** is intended to enrich students' vocabularies as well as to aid in the students' understanding of the play. Prior to each reading assignment, students will complete a two-part worksheet for 10 vocabulary words in the upcoming reading assignment. Part I focuses on students' use of general knowledge and contextual clues by giving the sentence in which the word appears in the text. Students are then to write down what they think the words mean based on the words' usage. Part II nails down the definitions of the words by giving students dictionary definitions of the words and having students match the words to the correct definitions based on the words' contextual usage. Students should then have an understanding of the words when they meet them in the text.

After each reading assignment, students will go back and formulate answers for the study guide questions. Discussion of these questions serves as a **review** of the most important events and ideas presented in the reading assignments.

After students complete reading the work, there is a **vocabulary review** lesson which pulls together all of the fragmented vocabulary lists for the reading assignments and gives students a review of all of the words they have studied.

Following the vocabulary review, a lesson is devoted to the **extra discussion questions/writing assignments**. These questions focus on interpretation, critical analysis and personal response, employing a variety of thinking skills and adding to the students' understanding of the play.

There are three **writing assignments** in this unit, each with the purpose of informing, persuading, or having students express personal opinions. In the first writing assignment, students will research Aristotle's elements of tragedy and relate them to *Oedipus Rex*. In the second writing assignment students will decide who is most at fault for the tragedy of Oedipus (fate/the gods, Iocaste, or Oedipus himself) and, using textual support, write a persuasive essay defending their position. Finally, students will create their own odes after examining/analyzing the four odes in *Oedipus Rex*.

There is a **nonfiction reading assignment**. Students must read nonfiction articles, books, etc. to gather information about the playwright, Sophocles.

The **review lesson** pulls together all of the aspects of the unit. The teacher is given several choices of activities or games to use which all serve the same basic function of reviewing all of the information presented in the unit.

The **unit test** comes in two formats: multiple choice or short answer. As a convenience, two different tests for each format have been included. There is also an advanced short answer unit test for advanced students.

There are additional **support materials** included with this unit. The **Unit Resource Materials** section includes suggestions for an in-class library, crossword and word search puzzles related to the play, and extra worksheets. There is a list of **bulletin board ideas** which gives the teacher suggestions for bulletin boards to go along with this unit. In addition, there is a list of **extra class activities** the teacher could choose from to enhance the unit or as a substitution for an exercise the teacher might feel is inappropriate for his/her class. **Answer keys** are located directly after the **reproducible student materials** throughout the unit. The **Vocabulary Resource Materials** section includes similar worksheets and games to reinforce the vocabulary words.

The **level** of this unit can be varied depending upon the criteria on which the individual assignments are graded, the teacher's expectations of his/her students in class discussions, and the formats chosen for the study guides, quizzes and test. If teachers have other ideas/activities they wish to use, they can usually easily be inserted prior to the review lesson.

The student materials may be reproduced for use in the teacher's classroom without infringement of copyrights. No other portion of this unit may be reproduced without the written consent of Teacher's Pet Publications, Inc.

UNIT OBJECTIVES
Oedipus Rex

1. Through reading Sophocles' *Oedipus Rex*, students will learn about the history of Greek Theatre and the structure of a Greek Tragedy, as well as the life of the playwright, Sophocles.

2. Students will demonstrate their understanding of the text on four levels: factual, interpretive, critical, and personal.

3. Students will explore the themes of *fear of the future, illusion vs. reality,* and *fate vs. free will.*

4. Students will be given the opportunity to practice reading both aloud and silently to improve their skills in each area.

5. Students will answer questions to demonstrate their knowledge and understanding of the main events and characters in *Oedipus Rex* as they relate to the playwright's theme development.

6. Students will enrich their vocabularies and improve their understanding of the play through the vocabulary lessons prepared for use in conjunction with the play.

7. The writing assignments in this unit are geared to several purposes:
    a. To have students demonstrate their abilities to inform, to persuade, or to express their own personal ideas
    Note: Students will demonstrate ability to write effectively to <u>inform</u> by developing and organizing facts to convey information. Students will demonstrate the ability to write effectively to <u>persuade</u> by selecting and organizing relevant information, establishing an argumentative purpose, and by designing an appropriate strategy for an identified audience. Students will demonstrate the ability to write effectively to <u>express personal ideas</u> by selecting a form and its appropriate elements.
    b. To check the students' reading comprehension
    c. To make students think about the ideas presented by the play
    d. To encourage logical thinking
    e. To provide an opportunity to practice good grammar and improve students' use of the English language.

8. Students will read aloud, report, and participate in large and small group discussions to improve their public speaking and personal interaction skills.

READING ASSIGNMENT SHEET
Oedipus Rex

Date Assigned	Scenes Assigned	Date Completed
	Prologue and Parodos	
	Scene 1 and Ode 1	
	Scene 2 and Ode 2	
	Scene 3 and Ode 3	
	Scene 4 and Ode 4	
	Exodos	

UNIT OUTLINE
Oedipus Rex

1	2	3	4	5
Greek Mythology: Background of the Oedipus Myth (The Riddle of the Sphinx) Intro to Greek Theatre PVR Prologue and Parodos	Study ? Prologue and Parodos PVR Scene 1/ Ode 1 Media center visit: non-fiction assignment: the life of Sophocles	Study ?s Scene 1/Ode 1 Read aloud/perform Prologue-Ode 1 PVR Scene/Ode 2	Study ?s Scene 2/Ode 2 Quiz: Prologue-Ode 1 Define ode and read Keats' "Ode to a Nightingale" PVR Scene3/ Ode 3	Study ?s Scene 3/Ode 3 Read aloud/perform Scene 2-Ode 3 PVR Scene/Ode 4
6	**7**	**8**	**9**	**10**
Study ?s Scene 4/Ode 4 Quiz: Scene/Odes 2 and 3 Characterization posters PVR Exodos	Study ?s Exodos Media center visit: Writing Assignment #1 Aristotle's Elements of Tragedy	Read aloud/ perform Scene 4-Exodos	Quiz: Scene 4-Exodos Dramatic Irony Exercise	Odes - examine Odes 1-4 for figurative language Writing Assignment #2
11	**12**	**13**	**14**	**15**
Mask Making Continue work on odes	Vocabulary Review	Group Work: Extra Discussion Questions	Writing Assignment#3 Persuasion Piece: Who is to Blame?	Peer Editing: Persuasion Piece: Who is to Blame?
16	**17**	**18**	**19**	**20**
Presentation of Odes	Presentation of Odes	Review Materials	Unit Test	

Key: P = Preview Study Questions   V = Vocabulary Work   R= Read

STUDY GUIDE QUESTIONS

SHORT ANSWER STUDY GUIDE QUESTIONS – Oedipus Rex

Prologue and Parodos:
1. What has been happening in Thebes that brings all members of the community to Oedipus's palace for answers?
2. What deed had Oedipus accomplished that makes the people believe that he is "the man surest in mortal ways/And wisest in the ways of God"?
3. What do the people of Thebes want Oedipus to do for them?
4. Who is Creon?
5. Who does Oedipus send to Delphi to learn how to save Thebes?
6. What suggestion does Creon make when Oedipus asks about the message from the god, Apollo?
7. Who is Laios?
8. Why has no one made an attempt to find out the truth about what had happened to Laois?
9. To which three gods does the Chorus pray for help?
10. What does the Chorus want the gods to do for them?

Scene 1 and Ode 1:
1. What promise does Oedipus make to anyone who comes forward with information about Laios's murder?
2. Why does Oedipus berate his people with regard to King Laios?
3. Who does the Choragos suggest could help Oedipus locate the whereabouts of the murderer?
4. When Oedipus asks the prophet to reveal the name of the murderer, what is the prophet's response?
5. What conclusion does Oedipus jump to when the prophet continually refuses to give specific information about the events surrounding the death of King Laios?
6. Who does the prophet finally reveal as the murderer of King Laios?
7. Who is said to be most concerned with the fate of Laios's murder?
8. Who does Oedipus accuse of being behind a plot to destroy him?
9. Who does the Chorus say will follow the killer wherever he goes?
10. What seems to be the attitude of the Chorus in Ode I toward the prophet's revelation?

Scene 2 and Ode 2:
1. Why is Creon upset at the opening of scene 2?
2. What is Creon's defense against the accusations against him?
3. Who does the Choragos claim can settle the dispute between Oedipus and Creon?
4. What convinces Oedipus to allow Creon to leave?
5. What "proof" does Iocaste offer that prophets do not tell the truth?
6. What is Oedipus's reaction to hearing that Laios was killed in a place where three highways met?
7. What has become of the only surviving member of the attack on King Laios's party?
8. Why had Oedipus fled Corinth many years before?
9. Who does Oedipus insist Iocaste send for?
10. According to Ode II, what can be said about the hearts of mortals?

Oedipus Rex Study Questions page 2

Scene 3 and Ode 3:
1. To whom does Iocaste make an offering?
2. What news does the messenger from Corinth bring to Thebes?
3. How does Oedipus react to the Corinthian messenger's news?
4. How did Polybos die?
5. Who does Oedipus claim to still fear in Corinth?
6. Specifically, what is Oedipus afraid of in Corinth?
7. What revelation does the messenger make to Oedipus?
8. How did Polybos come to raise Oedipus as his own son?
9. Who begs Oedipus to forget about finding the truth of his parentage?
10. Upon what mountain had the infant Oedipus been found?

Scene 4 and Ode 4:
1. Who identifies the old shepherd as the man who spared the infant Oedipus?
2. Where does the shepherd say he'd tended his sheep?
3. How did the shepherd and the messenger from Corinth know each other?
4. How does the shepherd react when the messenger states that King Oedipus was the baby the shepherd had given him?
5. How does Oedipus react to the shepherd's reluctance to speak?
6. Who had originally given the infant to the shepherd?
7. Why had the infant been handed over to the shepherd to begin with?
8. Why didn't the shepherd destroy the infant as instructed?
9. What truth does Oedipus learn?
10. Whose "great days [are] like ghosts gone"?

Exodos:
1. What news does the second messenger bring?
2. What did the messenger claim to have heard beyond the locked doors to the Queen's apartment?
3. What took the messenger's attention away from the din in the Queen's room?
4. What happens to Iocaste?
5. What did Oedipus do after he held Iocaste in his arms?
6. What does Oedipus claim he will do now that the truth is known?
7. Who does Oedipus blame for his fate?
8. Who takes over as the ruler of Thebes?
9. Who has been sent for to say good-bye to Oedipus?
10. What finally becomes of Oedipus?

ANSWER KEY SHORT ANSWER STUDY GUIDE QUESTIONS – *Oedipus Rex*

Prologue and Parodos:

1. What has been happening in Thebes that brings all members of the community to Oedipus's palace for answers?
    Plants and crops are dying, cattle and sheep are sick, unborn children are dying, and Thebes is becoming a wasteland.

2. What deed had Oedipus accomplished that makes the people believe that he is "the man surest in mortal ways/And wisest in the ways of God"?
    He saved Thebes from the Sphinx.

3. What do the people of Thebes want Oedipus to do for them?
    They want Oedipus to save them from their troubled times and "restore life to [the] city."

4. Who is Creon?
    Creon is the son of Menoikeus, brother of the Queen.

5. Who does Oedipus send to Delphi to learn how to save Thebes?
    Oedipus sends Creon to Apollo's temple at Delphi to learn how to save Thebes.

6. What suggestion does Creon make when Oedipus asks about the message from the god, Apollo?
    Creon suggests that he and Oedipus go someplace private to talk, but Oedipus insists that Creon speak publicly.

7. Who is Laios?
    Laios was the King of Thebes before Oedipus arrived.

8. Why has no one made an attempt to find out the truth about what had happened to Laois?
    The people of Thebes were too busy dealing with the Sphinx to investigate what had happened to Laios.

9. To which three gods does the Chorus pray for help?
    They pray to Athena, Artemis, and Apollo.

10. What does the Chorus want the gods to do for them?
    They want the gods to destroy their enemy and restore Thebes.

Scene 1 and Ode 1:

1. What promise does Oedipus make to anyone who comes forward with information about Laios's murder?
   He promises that no harm will come to the person who comes forward even if he has kept silent out of fear.

2. Why does Oedipus berate his people with regard to King Laios?
   If there had been no command from the Oracle, they would have allowed the murderer of King Laios to go unpunished.

3. Who does the Choragos suggest could help Oedipus locate the whereabouts of the murderer?
   The Choragos suggests the Oedipus send for the blind prophet Teiresias.

4. When Oedipus asks the prophet to reveal the name of the murderer, what is the prophet's response?
   Teiresias says that he has known all along, but he has made himself forget because he thinks it is better that no one knows.

5. What conclusion does Oedipus jump to when the prophet continually refuses to give specific information about the events surrounding the death of King Laios?
   Oedipus believes that Teiresias must be in on the murder of Laios.

6. Who does the prophet finally reveal as the murderer of King Laios?
   Teiresias claims that Oedipus murdered King Laios.

7. Who is said to be most concerned with the fate of Laios's murder?
   Apollo

8. Who does Oedipus accuse of being behind a plot to destroy him?
   Oedipus blames his brother-in-law Creon of plotting to destroy him.

9. Who does the Chorus say will follow the killer wherever he goes?
   The Furies will follow the killer wherever he goes.

10. What seems to be the attitude of the Chorus in Ode I towards the prophet's revelation?
    The Chorus says that it cannot believe "these evil words" and that Teiresias is lying.

Scene 2 and Ode 2:

1. Why is Creon upset at the opening of scene 2?
    Oedipus has accused him of being a traitor.

2. What is Creon's defense against the accusations against him?
    Why would he want the stress of being King when he already has the benefits as the King's brother-in-law without all the worries.

3. Who does the Choragos claim can settle the dispute between Oedipus and Creon?
    The Choragos claims that Iocaste, Oedipus's queen as well as Creon's sister, can settle the dispute.

4. What convinces Oedipus to allow Creon to leave?
    The Choragos says that life in Thebes is bad enough without having to deal with the feud between Oedipus and Creon.

5. What "proof" does Iocaste offer that prophets do not tell the truth?
    Iocaste tells Oedipus, Laios was told that he would be murdered by his own son. To avoid the prophecy, they'd left their infant son to die in the mountains; therefore, Teiresias's accusations against Oedipus cannot possibly be true.

6. What is Oedipus's reaction to hearing that Laios was killed in a place where three highways met?
    Oedipus remembers an altercation he'd had many years ago at that same location.

7. What has become of the only surviving member of the attack on King Laios's party?
    After learning that Laios's crown had been given to Oedipus, the servant had begged Iocaste to send him "as far away from the city" as she could send him.

8. Why had Oedipus fled Corinth many years before?
    An oracle had told Oedipus that he was fated to kill his father and breed children with his own mother. He left Corinth to avoid this.

9. Who does Oedipus insist Iocaste send for?
    Oedipus insists Iocaste send for her former slave who was a witness to the murder of King Laios.

10. According to Ode II, what can be said about the hearts of mortals?
    The Chorus claim mortals no longer know Apollo, and reverence for the gods has died away.

Scene 3 and Ode 3:

1. To whom does Iocaste make an offering?
   Iocaste makes an offering to Apollo.

2. What news does the messenger from Corinth bring to Thebes?
   Polybos, the King of Corinth is dead, and Oedipus is to be crowned King of Corinth.

3. How does Oedipus react to the Corinthian messenger's news?
   He reacts with relief because the prophecy had claimed that he would one day kill his father.

4. How did Polybos die?
   He died of old age.

5. Who does Oedipus claim to still fear in Corinth?
   He is still afraid of his mother, Merope, the wife of Polybos.

6. Specifically, what is Oedipus afraid of in Corinth?
   The prophecy claims he will marry his mother and the two will bear children.

7. What revelation does the messenger make to Oedipus?
   The messenger tells Oedipus that Polybos was not his biological father.

8. How did Polybos come to raise Oedipus as his own son?
   A shepherd brought the infant to the messenger now speaking to Oedipus, and he in turn gave the infant to the childless King and Queen of Corinth to raise.

9. Who begs Oedipus to forget about finding the truth of his parentage?
   Iocaste begs Oedipus to forget about the idea of learning his parentage.

10. Upon what mountain had the infant Oedipus been found?
    He had been left in the shadow of Mt. Kithairon in between Thebes and Corinth.

Scene 4 and Ode 4:

1. Who identifies the old shepherd as the man who spared the infant Oedipus?
   The messenger from Corinth recognizes the old shepherd as the man who had given him the infant Oedipus.

2. Where does the shepherd say he'd tended his sheep?
   He claims to have tended his sheep at Mt. Kithairon.

3. How did the shepherd and the messenger from Corinth know each other?
   They had spent three seasons tending their flocks together on Mt. Kithairon.

4. How does the shepherd react when the messenger states that King Oedipus was the baby the shepherd had given him?
   The old shepherd tells the Corinthian messenger to hold his tongue.

5. How does Oedipus react to the shepherd's reluctance to speak?
   An angry Oedipus threatens to kill the shepherd if he doesn't talk.

6. Who had originally given the infant to the shepherd?
   Iocaste

7. Why had the infant been handed over to the shepherd to begin with?
   A prophecy had claimed the child would grow to kill his father and marry his mother. Laios and Iocaste were trying to avoid the fulfillment of the prophecy.

8. Why didn't the shepherd destroy the infant as instructed?
   He'd pitied the baby, and gave it to the man from Corinth. The shepherd figured the baby would be far enough, away and no one would discover that he'd let the child live.

9. What truth does Oedipus learn?
   He learns that he was the infant who grew up and killed King Laios (his father) at a crossroads after leaving Corinth, and that he unwittingly married his own mother after solving the Sphinx's riddle. She also bore him four children: two sons and two daughters.

10. Whose "great days [are] like ghosts gone"?
    Oedipus's

Exodos:

1. What news does the second messenger bring?
   He brings word that Queen Iocaste is dead.

2. What does the messenger claim to have heard beyond the locked doors to the Queen's apartment?
   He hears her screaming some absurdities about King Laios and Oedipus, but he could not understand her.

3. What takes the messenger's attention away from the din in the Queen's room?
   Oedipus enters begging for a sword and curses his wife.

4. What happens to Iocaste?
    Iocaste hangs herself in her apartment.

5. What did Oedipus do after he held Iocaste in his arms?
    He takes the brooches from her dress and blinds himself with them.

6. What does Oedipus claim he will do now that the truth is known?
    He is going to follow his own edict and go into self-exile.

7. Who does Oedipus blame for his fate?
    Oedipus blames Apollo.

8. Who takes over as the ruler of Thebes?
    Creon

9. Who has been sent for to say good-bye to Oedipus?
    Creon sends for Oedipus's two daughters, Ismene and Antigone, to say good-bye to their father.

10. What finally becomes of Oedipus?
    He leaves Thebes to be exiled to the mountains of Kithairon where he should have died as an infant.

STUDY GUIDE/QUIZ QUESTIONS – *Oedipus Rex*
Multiple Choice Format

Prologue and Parodos:

1. What has been happening in Thebes that brings all members of the community to Oedipus's palace for answers?
    A. A terrible beast, a Sphinx, has been terrifying the city.
    B. A raging volcano has sent rivers of lava through the streets.
    C. A plague has descended upon the entire city; death and decay is everywhere.
    D. Gigantic swarms of locusts have descended upon the city.

2. What deed had Oedipus accomplished that makes the people believe that he is "the man surest in mortal ways/And wisest in the ways of God"?
    A. He'd solved the riddle of the Sphinx and it killed itself.
    B. He had defeated the Cretan Bull.
    C. He killed the Nemean Lion.
    D. He killed the Lernean Hydra, a nine headed monster.

3. What do the people of Thebes want Oedipus to do for them?
    A. They blame him for the problems and want him to leave town.
    B. They want him to rid Thebes of the problems and restore the city.
    C. They want him to make a sacrifice to Zeus to appease the gods.
    D. They want him to offer his youngest daughter to the fiery volcano.

4. Who is Creon?
    A. He is Oedipus's brother and second in command in Thebes.
    B. He is Oedipus's eldest son.
    C. He is Iocaste's, Oedipus's wife's brother.
    D. He is a priest at the temple of Delphi.

5. Who does Oedipus send to Delphi to learn how to save Thebes?
    A. Iocaste
    B. Creon
    C. Laios
    D. Antigone

6. What suggestion does Creon make when Oedipus asks about the message from the god, Apollo?
    A. Creon suggests that they make a sacrifice to Apollo as soon as possible.
    B. Creon suggests that Oedipus himself make a pilgrimage to Delphi.
    C. Creon suggests that they create stone levis to keep the lava out of the streets.
    D. Creon suggests that they talk privately somewhere about the god's message.

7. Who is Laios?
   A. He is Oedipus's eldest son.
   B. He is Creon's brother.
   C. He is Iocaste's first husband.
   D. He is a prophet.

8. No one attempted to find out the truth about what had happened to Laois because:
   A. they were too busy trying to defeat the Sphinx that was terrifying Thebes.
   B. they thought they already knew the truth.
   C. Iocaste told the people that she was distraught enough without learning more.
   D. everyone who tried to learn the truth ended up dead.

9. To which three gods does the Chorus pray for help?
   A. They pray to Zeus, Hermes, and Apollo.
   B. They pray to Athena, Artemis, and Apollo.
   C. They pray to Zeus, Poseidon, and Apollo.
   D. They pray to Athena, Zeus, and Apollo.

10. The Chorus wants the gods to:
    A. destroy whatever enemy is bringing the plague upon Thebes.
    B. send them a hero to defend them.
    C. punish Oedipus for not following through on learning who murdered Laios.
    D. divert the molten lava away from Thebes.

Scene 1 and Ode 1:

1. What promise does Oedipus make to anyone who comes forward with information about Laios's murder?
    A. Oedipus will give a handsome reward of gold.
    B. He says that no harm will come to anyone who comes forward.
    C. He will give a formal pardon for the treason of withholding information.
    D. Oedipus makes no promises; he demands that anyone with information come forward.

2. Oedipus berates his people with regard to King Laios because:
    A. they gave the crown to Oedipus so soon after the king's death.
    B. they showed no respect for the king because they held no funeral rite in his honor.
    C. no statue was erected in King Laios's memory.
    D. if the oracle had not commanded it, they would have ignored their king's murderer.

3. Who does the Choragos suggest could help Oedipus locate the whereabouts of the murderer?
    A. Creon
    B. Teiresias
    C. Iocaste
    D. Apollo

4. When Oedipus asks the prophet to reveal the name of the murderer, what is the prophet's response?
    A. Although Teiresias knows the answer, it is better that no one else ever learns the truth.
    B. The king was never murdered at all; he is still alive in another land.
    C. He claims that Iocaste murdered her husband.
    D. He claims that he does not know because Apollo has kept the name from him.

5. What conclusion does Oedipus jump to when the prophet continually refuses to give specific information about the events surrounding the death of King Laios?
    A. Teiresias is a false prophet and has created prophecies for gold.
    B. The prophet is really King Laios in disguise.
    C. Teriesias must have been in on the plot to kill Laios.
    D. Teriesias is lying to cover up the fact that he has no prophetic powers.

6. Who does the prophet finally reveal as the murderer of King Laios?
    A. Iocaste
    B. Creon
    C. Teiresias
    D. Oedipus

7. Who is said to be most concerned with the fate of Laios's murder?
    A. Apollo
    B. Teiresias
    C. Iocaste
    D. Creon

8. Who does Oedipus accuse of being behind a plot to destroy him?
    A. Iocaste
    B. Teiresias
    C. Apollo
    D. Creon

9. Who does the Chorus say will follow the killer wherever he goes?
    A. the Fates
    B. the Furies
    C. Apollo
    D. Zeus

10. What seems to be the attitude of the Chorus in Ode I toward the prophet's revelation?
    A. They are respectful because he is a wise man and should be listened to.
    B. They are angry because the prophet has spoken evil words and lies.
    C. They are afraid because they know the prophet speaks only the truth.
    D. They are vengeful because they believe that he is in on the death of King Laios.

Scene 2 and Ode 2:

1. Why is Creon upset at the opening of scene 2?
    A. Oedipus has accused him of treason.
    B. King Laios was never given a proper burial.
    C. Iocaste believes that he is plotting against her husband.
    D. Teiresias has foretold an evil omen for Creon.

2. What is Creon's defense against the accusations against him?
    A. He claims that Laios's body was never returned to Thebes, so he could not have given Laios a proper burial.
    B. He says that he would never do anything to cause his sister, Iocaste, any pain.
    C. Why would he want the stress of being king when he already enjoys the same perks?
    D. He claims that Teiresias is a liar, and that his fate is his own; no evil awaits him.

3. Who does the Choragos claim can settle the dispute between Oedipus and Creon?
    A. Teiresias
    B. Apollo
    C. Zeus
    D. Iocaste

4. What convinces Oedipus to allow Creon to leave?
    A. The Choragos says that things are bad enough without the two of them fighting.
    B. He finally realizes that Creon is telling the truth.
    C. He did not have enough evidence against Creon, so he was forced to let him go.
    D. Iocaste begged for her brother's life and Oedipus relented.

5. What "proof" does Iocaste offer that prophets do not tell the truth?
    A. She had been told that she would marry her own son, but she'd killed the child.
    B. Her husband had been told that his own son would kill him, but he was killed by bandits at a crossroads.
    C. The rains never come exactly when they are predicted to.
    D. The gods create "fate" at their whim; the prophets cannot foresee the gods' intentions.

6. What is Oedipus's reaction to hearing that Laios was killed in a place where three highways met?
    A. He wants to go to the spot and search for clues to the murder.
    B. He remembers an altercation he once had in the some location.
    C. He is angry that a king would die in such an undignified manner.
    D. He wants to erect a monument at the place in Laios's memory.

7. What became of the only surviving member of the attack on King Laios's party?
    A. He hanged himself as soon as he returned.
    B. He became the leader of the new king's sentries.
    C. He begged Iocaste to send him as far from Thebes as possible.
    D. He was executed for failure to protect the king.

8. Why had Oedipus fled Corinth many years before?
    A. An oracle told him that he would kill his father and marry his mother.
    B. He had killed a man.
    C. He was wrongly accused of treason by King Polybos.
    D. He wanted to go out and explore the world.

9. Who does Oedipus insist Iocaste send for?
    A. She sends for Teiresias the prophet.
    B. She sends for brother Creon.
    C. She sends for the surviving member of Laios's entourage.
    D. She sends for the leader of the king's sentries.

10. According to Ode II, what can be said about the hearts of mortals?
    A. They are weak in fear of the gods.
    B. They are strong in faith.
    C. They are loyal to their leaders.
    D. They no longer know Apollo, and have lost reverence for the gods.

Scene 3 and Ode 3:

1. To whom does Iocaste make an offering?
    A. Zeus
    B. Aphrodite
    C. Apollo
    D. Artemis

2. What news does the messenger from Corinth bring to Thebes?
    A. The King of Corinth is preparing to make war on Thebes.
    B. A warrant has been issued for Oedipus's arrest for treason.
    C. Oedipus's father, wishes for his son to pay a visit.
    D. The King of Corinth is dead, and Oedipus is to be crowned King.

3. How does Oedipus react to the Corinthian messenger's news?
    A. He is fearful of being charged with treason against the Corinthian crown.
    B. He is filled with relief.
    C. He prepares for war with Corinth.
    D. He prepares to visit his father.

4. How did Polybos die?
    A. He was killed by his son.
    B. He was murdered by his wife.
    C. He died of old age.
    D. His death is shrouded in mystery.

5. Who does Oedipus claim to still fear in Corinth?
    A. He fears the family of the man he'd killed many years before.
    B. He fears Merope, the wife of Polybos.
    C. He fears the priest at the temple at Delphi.
    D. He fears the ghost of Polybos.

6. Specifically, what is Oedipus afraid of in Corinth?
    A. He is afraid that he will marry his mother and the two will bear children.
    B. He is afraid that he will be overcome by rage at being accused of treason.
    C. He is afraid that he will be executed for murder.
    D. He is afraid that he will be blamed for the death of the king.

7. What revelation does the messenger make to Oedipus?
    A. King Polybos's murderer has already been caught.
    B. Oedipus was born to a servant of the King of Corinth, not to his mother Merope.
    C. The messenger is really King Laios who had been in hiding from Creon for years.
    D. Polybos was not Oedipus's natural father.

8. How did Polybos come to raise Oedipus as his own son?
    A. Polybos is his father; it is natural that he would raise his son.
    B. Polybos found the abandoned infant Oedipus in the forest while out hunting.
    C. The messenger had been given an infant found in the mountains and he, in turn, gave the child to the king and queen.
    D. Although the illegitimate son of a servant girl, Polybos took the infant in when the girl died.

9. Who begs Oedipus to forget about finding the truth of his parentage?
    A. Creon
    B. Iocaste
    C. Teiresias
    D. the messenger from Corinth

10. Upon what mountain had the infant Oedipus been found?
    A. Mt. Kithairon
    B. Mt. Sinai
    C. Mt. Olympus
    D. Mt. Everest

Scene 4 and Ode 4:

1. Who identified the old shepherd as the man who spared the infant Oedipus?
   A. Iocaste
   B. Creon
   C. Teiresias
   D. the Corinthian messenger

2. Where did the shepherd say he'd tended his sheep?
   A. He tended them on Mt. Kithairon.
   B. He tended them in pastures between Corinth and Sparta.
   C. He tended them in pastures between Thebes and Athens.
   D. He tended them on Mt. Olympus.

3. How did the shepherd and the messenger from Corinth know each other?
   A. They are brothers.
   B. They'd tended their flocks together for three seasons.
   C. The old shepherd is the messenger's father.
   D. They'd both served in the king's guard.

4. How does the shepherd react when the messenger states that King Oedipus was the baby the shepherd had given him?
   A. He is surprised that the child had survived.
   B. He is repulsed by the fact that his king was of such a low birth.
   C. He tells the messenger to hold his tongue.
   D. He embraces Oedipus and weeps openly.

5. How does Oedipus react to the shepherd's reluctance to speak?
   A. He is sympathetic because the shepherd is so emotional about Oedipus's true identity.
   B. He becomes angry and threatens to kill the shepherd.
   C. He is insulted that a lowly shepherd would be repulsed by Oedipus's common birth.
   D. He threatens to banish the shepherd from Thebes forever.

6. Who had originally given the infant to the shepherd?
   A. Iocaste
   B. Laios
   C. Creon
   D. Teiresias

7. Why had the infant been handed over to the shepherd to begin with?
   A. He would grow to be more handsome than his own vain father.
   B. His poor parents could not afford to care for the child.
   C. It had been foretold that he would grow to kill his father and marry his mother.
   D. He was born with deformed feet and his parents did not want him.

8. The shepherd didn't destroy the infant as instructed because:
   A. it was his own child.
   B. he wanted to secretly raise the child to come back and take vengeance on the king.
   C. he thought he had; he did not know that the child survived.
   D. he pitied the infant and gave it to someone far away from Thebes.

9. What truth does Oedipus learn?
   A. The shepherd is his true father.
   B. Iocaste has been unfaithful and his children are really the shepherd's children.
   C. The prophecy was right; he killed his father (Laios) and married his mother (Iocaste).
   D. Merope, his mother, had an affair with Laios, and Laios is his true father.

10. Whose "great days [are] like ghosts gone"?
    A. Apollo's
    B. Oedipus's
    C. Iocaste's
    D. Creon's

Exodos:

1. What news does the second messenger bring?
    A. Oedipus's children have been killed.
    B. Merope has also died; the prophecy was wrong.
    C. Teiresias has been murdered by Iocaste.
    D. Iocaste is dead.

2. What did the messenger claim to have heard beyond the locked doors to the Queen's apartment?
    A. He heard her screaming some absurdities about King Laios and Oedipus, but he could not understand her.
    B. He heard a terrible fight between the Queen and the prophet Teiresias.
    C. He heard the Queen's screams as she was murdered by Teiresias.
    D. He heard the Queen smashing everything in the apartment.

3. What takes the messenger's attention away from the din in the Queen's room?
    A. Creon tries to break the door to the apartment down.
    B. Oedipus runs in calling for a sword and cursing his wife.
    C. The children, Polyneices, Eteocles, Antigone, and Ismene run screaming through the halls.
    D. There is a sudden, horrible silence in the room.

4. What happens to Iocaste?
    A. Oedipus strangles her.
    B. She hangs herself.
    C. Creon stabs her.
    D. She kills Teiresias because of his prophecies.

5. What does Oedipus do after he held Iocaste in his arms?
    A. He slit her throat.
    B. He cries and tells her that he forgave her everything.
    C. He pushes her roughly aside in disgust.
    D. He takes the brooches from her gown and blinds himself.

6. What does Oedipus claim he will do now that the truth is known?
    A. He will take his family and leave town.
    B. He will kill himself.
    C. He will exile himself just as he said he would do to the murderer of King Laios.
    D. He wants Creon to execute him.

7. Who does Oedipus blame for his fate?
    A. Apollo
    B. Iocaste
    C. Laios
    D. Creon

8. Who takes over as the ruler of Thebes?
    A. Teiresias
    B. Polyneices, Oedipus's son
    C. Creon
    D. Eteocles, Oedipus's son

9. Who had been sent for to say good-bye to Oedipus?
    A. Polyneices and Eteocles
    B. Polyneices, Eteocles, Antigone, and Ismene
    C. Creon
    D. Antigone and Ismene

10. What finally becomes of Oedipus?
    A. He lives in self-exile on Mt. Kithairon where he should have died as an infant.
    B. He is executed for treason.
    C. He hangs himself.
    D. He takes the crown in Corinth and the rightful king.

ANSWER KEY - MULTIPLE CHOICE STUDY/QUIZ QUESTIONS – *Oedipus Rex*

Prologue/Parodos	Scene 1/Ode 1	Scene 2/Ode 2	Scene 3/Ode 3
1. C	1. B	1. A	1. C
2. A	2. D	2. C	2. D
3. B	3. B	3. D	3. B
4. C	4. A	4. A	4. C
5. B	5. C	5. B	5. B
6. D	6. D	6. B	6. A
7. C	7. A	7. C	7. D
8. A	8. D	8. A	8. C
9. B	9. B	9. C	9. B
10. A	10. B	10. D	10. A

Scene 4/Ode 4	Exodos
1. D	1. D
2. A	2. A
3. B	3. B
4. C	4. B
5. B	5. D
6. A	6. C
7. C	7. A
8. D	8. C
9. C	9. D
10. B	10. A

PRE-READING VOCABULARY WORKSHEETS

VOCABULARY FOR THE PROLOGUE AND PARADOS – *Oedipus Rex*

Part I: Using Prior Knowledge and Contextual Clues

Below are the sentences in which the vocabulary words appear in the text. Read the sentence. Use any clues you can find in the sentence combined with your prior knowledge, and write what you think the underlined words mean on the lines provided.

1. "My children, generations of the living/In the line of Kadmos, nursed at his ancient **hearth**…"

   _____

2. "Why have you strewn yourselves before these altars/In **supplication**, with your boughs and garlands?"

   _____

3. "Death alone/**Battens** upon the misery of Thebes."

   _____

4. "Think how all men call you/**Liberator** for your triumph long ago."

   _____

5. "Once, years ago, with happy **augury**,/You brought us fortune; be the same again!"

   _____

6. "I should do ill/To **scant** whatever duty God reveals."

   _____

7. "The god commands us to expel from the land of Thebes/An old **defilement** we are sheltering."

   _____

8. "Strange, that a highwayman should be so daring--/Unless some **faction** here bribed him to do it."

   _____

Oedipus Rex Vocabulary Worksheet Prologue and Parados Continued

9. "It is most fitting that Apollo shows,/As you do, this ***compunction*** for the dead."

_____

10. "Send the ***besieger*** plunging from our homes/Into the vast sea-room of the Atlantic/Or into the waves that foam eastward of Thrace…"

_____

Part II: Determining the Meaning
   Match the vocabulary words to their dictionary definitions

   ____ 1. hearth   A. the floor of a fireplace, usually of stone, brick
   ____ 2. supplication   B. a group or clique within a larger group, party, government
   ____ 3. battens   C. to treat slightly or inadequately
   ____ 4. liberator   D. Someone who releases people from captivity or bondage
   ____ 5. augury   E. an enemy who lays siege to your position
   ____ 6. scant   F. to ask for humbly or earnestly, as by praying
   ____ 7. defilement   G. any uneasiness or hesitation about the rightness of an action
   ____ 8. faction   H. an event indicating important things to come; fortunetelling
   ____ 9. compunction   I. to thrive and prosper, especially at another's expense
   ____ 10. besieger   J. to make foul, dirty, or unclean; pollute

VOCABULARY FOR SCENE ONE AND ODE ONE – *Oedipus Rex*

Part I: Using Prior Knowledge and Contextual Clues

Below are the sentences in which the vocabulary words appear in the text. Read the sentence. Use any clues you can find in the sentence combined with your prior knowledge, and write what you think the underlined words mean on the lines provided.

1. "…if any man/Fearing for his friend or for himself disobeys this ***edict***,/Hear what I propose to do…"

    _____

2. "I solemnly forbid the people of this country/… ever to receive that man/Or speak to him, no matter who he is, or let him/Join in sacrifice, ***lustration***, or in prayer."

    _____

3. "Now I,/Having the power that he held before me,/Having his bed, ***begetting*** his children there/Upon his wife, as he would have, had he lived…"

    _____

4. "Apollo, when we sent to him,/Sent us back word that this great ***pestilence***/Would lift, but only if we established clearly/The identity of those who murdered Laios."

    _____

5. "Can you use/…any art of divination/To purify yourself, and Thebes, and me/From this ***contagion***?"

    _____

6. "When it comes to speech, your own is neither temperate/Nor opportune. I wish to be more ***prudent***."

    _____

7. "Can you possible think you have/Some way of going free, after such ***insolence***?"

    _____

Oedipus Rex Vocabulary Worksheet Scene 1 and Ode 1 Continued

8. "He has brought this ***decrepit*** fortune-teller, this/Collector of dirty pennies, this prophet fraud–/Why he is not more clairvoyant than I am!"

_____

9. "Tell us;/Has your ***mummery*** ever approached the truth?"

_____

10. "The Delphic stone of prophecies/Remembers ancient ***regicide***/And a still bloody hand."

_____

Part II: Determining the Meaning
   Match the vocabulary words to their dictionary definitions

   ____ 1. edict   A. wise or judicious in practical affairs
   ____ 2. lustration   B. fathering; siring
   ____ 3. begetting   C. the killing of a king
   ____ 4. pestilence   D. rude or impertinent behavior or speech
   ____ 5. contagion   E. the act of purifying by means of ceremony
   ____ 6. prudent   F. something that is considered harmful, destructive, or evil
   ____ 7. insolence   G. any performance or ceremony regarded as absurd or false
   ____ 8. decrepit   H. any authoritative proclamation or command
   ____ 9. mummery   I. the means by which a contagious disease is transmitted
   ____ 10. regicide   J. weakened by old age; feeble

VOCABULARY FOR SCENE TWO AND ODE TWO – *Oedipus Rex*

Part I: Using Prior Knowledge and Contextual Clues

Below are the sentences in which the vocabulary words appear in the text. Read the sentence. Use any clues you can find in the sentence combined with your prior knowledge, and write what you think the underlined words mean on the lines provided.

1. "Why? How ***brazen*** of you to come to my house,/You murderer!"

_____

2. "But… the ***enquiry***?/I suppose you held one?"
   "We did, but we learned nothing."

_____

3. "No, I have not gone mad; I need no honors,/Except those with the ***perquisites*** I have now."

_____

4. "But is he not quick in his duplicity?/And shall I not be quick to ***parry*** him?"

_____

5. "Poor foolish men, what wicked ***din*** is this?"

_____

6. "There was suspicion without evidence; yet it ***rankled***/As even false charges will."

_____

7. "He would not commit himself to such a charge,/But he has brought in that damnable ***soothsayer***/To tell his story."

_____

8. "At a feast, a drunken man ***maundering*** in his cups/Cries out that I am not my father's son!"

_____

Oedipus Rex Vocabulary Worksheet Scene 2 and Ode 2 Continued

9. "I must be shunned by all. And I myself/Pronounced this **_malediction_** upon myself!"

_____

10. "Rather let me vanish from the race of men/Than know the **_abomination_** destined me!"

_____

Part II: Determining the Meaning
    Match the vocabulary words to their dictionary definitions

    ____ 1. brazen   A. a loud, disturbing noise
    ____ 2. enquiry   B. anything greatly disliked or abhorred
    ____ 3. perquisites   C. to turn aside; evade or dodge
    ____ 4. parry   D. person who professes to foretell events, fortune-teller
    ____ 5. din   E. moving or acting in an aimless or vague manner
    ____ 6. rankled   F. those things claimed as exclusive rights
    ____ 7. soothsayer   G. shameless or impudent
    ____ 8. maundering   H. a seeking or request for truth, information, or knowledge
    ____ 9. malediction   I. caused keen irritation or bitter resentment
    ____ 10. abomination   J. the utterance of a curse

VOCABULARY FOR SCENE THREE AND ODE THREE – *Oedipus Rex*

Part I: Using Prior Knowledge and Contextual Clues

Below are the sentences in which the vocabulary words appear in the text. Read the sentence. Use any clues you can find in the sentence combined with your prior knowledge, and write what you think the underlined words mean on the lines provided.

1. "Princes of Thebes, it has occurred to me/To visit the altars of the gods, bearing/These branches as a ***suppliant***, and this incense."

   _____

2. "…his noble soul is ***overwrought*** with fantasies of dread,/Else he would consider/The new prophecies in the light of the old."

   _____

3. "Our hearts are heavy with fear/When we see our leader distracted, as helpless sailors/Are terrified by the confusion of their ***helmsman***."

   _____

4. "The word is that the people of the ***Isthmus***/Intend to call Oedipus to be their king."

   _____

5. "Death holds him in his ***sepulcher***."

   _____

6. "Listen to what this man says, and then tell me/What has become of the ***solemn*** prophecies."

   _____

7. "As for that/You must be ***reassured*** by the news I gave you."

   _____

8. "Can you not see that all your fears are ***groundless***?"

   _____

Oedipus Rex Vocabulary Worksheet Scene 3 and Ode 3 Continued

9. "You need not worry. Suppose my mother a slave,/And born of slaves: no **_baseness_** can touch you."

_____

10. "Of the **_nymphs_** that flower beyond the years,/Who bore you, royal child,/To Pan of the hills or the timberline Apollo…?"

_____

Part II: Determining the Meaning
    Match the vocabulary words to their dictionary definitions

____ 1. suppliant   A. without rational basis
____ 2. overwrought   B. one who asks humbly and earnestly
____ 3. helmsman   C. characteristic of or befitting an inferior person or thing
____ 4. Isthmus   D. a tomb, grave, or burial place
____ 5. sepulcher   E. Female spirits in forests, bodies of water, and other natural places
____ 6. solemn   F. causing serious thoughts or a grave mood
____ 7. reassured   G. restored confidence to
____ 8. groundless   H. a person who steers a ship
____ 9. baseness   I. extremely or excessively excited or agitated
____ 10. nymphs   J. a narrow strip of land, bordered on both sides by water, connecting two larger bodies of land

VOCABULARY FOR SCENE 4 AND ODE 4 – *Oedipus Rex*

Part I: Using Prior Knowledge and Contextual Clues

Below are the sentences in which the vocabulary words appear in the text. Read the sentence. Use any clues you can find in the sentence combined with your prior knowledge, and write what you think the underlined words mean on the lines provided.

1. "I was a shepherd most of my life."
   "Where mainly did you go for **_pasturage_**?"
   _____

2. "…if you are what this man says you are,/No man living is more **_wretched_** than Oedipus."
   _____

3. "What measure shall I give these generations/That breathe on the **_void_** and are void/And exist and do not exist?"
   _____

4. "Your **_splendor_** is all fallen."
   _____

5. "No prince in Thebes had ever such **_renown_**,/No prince won such grade of power."
   _____

6. "The great door that **_expelled_** you to the light/Gave at night—ah, gave night to your glory: As to the father, to the fathering son."
   _____

7. "How could that queen whom Laios won,/the garden that he **_harrowed_** at his height,/Be silent when that act was done?"
   _____

8. "Though never willed, though far down the deep past,/You bed, your dread **_sirings_**,/Are brought to book at last."
   _____

edipus Rex Vocabulary Worksheet Scene 4 and Ode 4 Continued

9. "That with my wailing lips I take to cry:/For I weep the world's **outcast**./I was blind, and now I can tell why…"

_____

10. "I was blind, and now I can tell why:/Asleep, for you had given **ease** of breath/To Thebes, while the false years went by."

_____

Part II: Determining the Meaning
    Match the vocabulary words to their dictionary definitions

____ 1. pasturage   A. broke up soil with a tool made of a heavy frame with sharp teeth
____ 2. wretched   B. brilliant or gorgeous appearance
____ 3. void   C. the activity or business of pasturing livestock
____ 4. splendor   D. freedom from difficulty or great effort
____ 5. renown   E. forced or drove out
____ 6. expelled   F. one who is rejected or discarded
____ 7. harrowed   G. widespread and high repute; fame
____ 8. sirings   H. an empty space; emptiness
____ 9. outcast   I. very unfortunate in condition or circumstances
____ 10. ease   J. a father's children

VOCABULARY FOR EXODOS – *Oedipus Rex*

Part I: Using Prior Knowledge and Contextual Clues

Below are the sentences in which the vocabulary words appear in the text. Read the sentence. Use any clues you can find in the sentence combined with your prior knowledge, and write what you think the underlined words mean on the lines provided.

1. "…What horrors are yours to see and hear, what weight/Of sorrow to be endured, if, true to your birth,/You **_venerate_** the line of Labdakos!"

   _____

2. "…Oedipus burst in moaning and would not let us/Keep **_vigil_** to the end…"

   _____

3. "…the King ripped from her gown the golden **_brooches_**/That were her ornament, and raised them, and plunged them down/Straight into his own eyeballs…'"

   _____

4. "O, cloud of night,/Never to be turned away; night coming on,/I can not tell how: night like a **_shroud_**!"

   _____

5. "Oh child of evil,/To have entered that wretched bed—the selfsame one!/More **_primal_** than sin itself, this fell to me."

   _____

6. "Why did I not die? Then I should never/Have shown the world my **_execrable_** birth."

   _____

7. "But his command is plain: the **_parricide_**/Must be destroyed. I am that evil man."

   _____

8. "…Where is the man, my daughters, who would dare/Risk the **_bane_** that lies on all my children?"

   _____

Oedipus Rex Vocabulary Worksheet Exodos Continued

9. "Let every man in mankind's *__frailty__*/Consider his last day…"

_____

10. "…and let none/***Presume*** on his good fortune until he find/Life, at his death, a memory without pain."

_____

Part II: Determining the Meaning
    Match the vocabulary words to their dictionary definitions

    ____ 1. venerate   A. relatively large decorative pins or clasps
    ____ 2. vigil   B. a person or thing that ruins or spoils
    ____ 3. brooches   C. being first in time; original
    ____ 4. shroud   D. moral weakness; liability to yield to temptation
    ____ 5. primal   E. a period of watchful attention maintained at night
    ____ 6. execrable   F. utterly detestable; abominable; very bad
    ____ 7. parricide   G. to take for granted, assume, or suppose
    ____ 8. bane   H. a cloth or sheet in which a corpse is wrapped for burial
    ____ 9. frailty   I. a person who kills his own parent
    ____ 10. presume   J. to regard or treat with reverence or respect

VOCABULARY ANSWER KEY – *Oedipus Rex*

Prologue/Parodos
1. A
2. F
3. I
4. D
5. H
6. C
7. J
8. B
9. G
10. E

Scene 1/Ode 1
1. H
2. E
3. B
4. F
5. I
6. A
7. D
8. J
9. G
10. C

Scene 2/Ode 2
1. G
2. H
3. F
4. C
5. A
6. I
7. D
8. E
9. J
10. B

Scene 3/Ode 3
1. B
2. I
3. H
4. J
5. D
6. F
7. G
8. A
9. C
10. E

Scene 4/Ode 4
1. C
2. I
3. H
4. B
5. G
6. E
7. A
8. J
9. F
10. D

Exodos
1. J
2. E
3. A
4. H
5. C
6. F
7. I
8. B
9. D
10. G

DAILY LESSONS

LESSON ONE

Objectives
1. To become familiar with the Greek myth surrounding Oedipus and The Sphinx and its connection to Sophocles' tragedy
2. To create riddles much like those of the Sphinx
3. To introduce to Sophocles's tragedy, *Oedipus Rex* and the structure of a Greek Tragedy
4. To distribute books, study questions, and other related materials
5. To preview the vocabulary worksheet and study guide questions for the Prologue and Parodos
6. To read the Prologue and Parodos

Activity #1

Read the story of Oedipus and the Sphinx (easily downloaded from the Internet). Ask students what character traits Oedipus demonstrated through his interaction with the Sphinx. Write these traits on the front board and ask students to support them with details from the story. Next, ask students to compose their own riddles, using the Riddle of the Sphinx as a model (you might also use examples of riddles from chapter 5 of J. R. R. Tolkein's *The Hobbit* if you happen to have a copy). My students love this activity and actually do a good job with creating a rhyme scheme. Give bonus points to those students who can stump their peers with a solid riddle, as well as bonus points for those who are able to solve the riddles of their peers. Some examples of student riddles are below:

It can hold things
Yet it can let them slip away
It is an entrance
But it is an exit, some say
You cannot see in one
Yet sometimes see through it you may
    (answer: a hole) by Heather M.

I have feet, but I cannot walk;
I have chords but can never talk;
You can play me and never win;
I was once living but never had skin.
    (answer: a piano) by Kevin K.

I broaden your mind every night
I don't give up without a fight
Without me, the mornings aren't very funny
I am like your energizer bunny
    (answer: sleep) by Alex G.

What is, oh, so bright
And turns on when day becomes night?
It is also a decoration
That helps with your notations.
    (answer: a lamp) by Stephanie R.

What does man love more than life,
Fear more than death or mortal strife,
What the poor have, the rich require,
And what contented men desire,
What the miser spends and the spendthrift saves,
All men carry it to their graves
    (answer: nothing) by Sandy R.

I fly through the air
Due to a blow,
My dimples are showing,
I am the color of snow.
    (answer: a golf ball) by Leah K.

<u>Activity #2</u>
    Ask students to brainstorm what the term "tragedy" means, and try to come up with what elements of any plot could be considered as "tragic." Have students share ideas aloud and write them on the chalk board. Ask students to brainstorm examples of tragedies from both literature and real life. List them on the board and discuss what makes each of these stories tragic. What do they all seem to have in common? Lead into discussion of the elements of a tragedy (see below).

    A Greek tragedy is structures as follows:
    I. **Prologue:** Spoken by one or two characters before the chorus appears. The prologue usually gives the background information needed to understand the events of the play.
    II. **Parodos:** the song sung by the chorus as it makes its entrance
    III. **Episodes/Scenes:** the main action of the play
    IV. **Odes:** a song (and often dance) that reflects on the events of the episodes, and weaves the plot into a cohesive whole
        A. *Choragos:* the leader of the chorus who often interacts with the characters in the scenes
        B. *Chorus:* the singers/dancers who remark on the action
            1. strophe: the movement of the chorus from right to left across the stage
            2. antistrophe: the reaction to the strophe, which moves across the stage from left to right.
    V. **Paean:** a prayer of thanksgiving to Dionysus in whose honor the Greek plays were performed
    VI. **Exodos:** sung by the chorus as it makes its final exit, which usually offers words of wisdom related to the actions and outcome of the play

<u>Activity #3</u>
    Distribute the materials students will use in this unit. Explain in detail how students are to use these materials.

    <u>Study Guides</u> Students should read the study guide questions for each reading assignment prior to beginning the reading assignment to get a feeling for what events and ideas are important in the section they are about to read. After reading the section, students will (as a class or individually)

answer the questions to review the important events and ideas from that section of the play. Students should keep the study guides as study materials for the unit test.

Vocabulary   Prior to each reading assignment, students will do vocabulary work related to the section of the work they are about to read. Following the completion of the reading of the play, there will be a vocabulary review of all the words used in the vocabulary assignments. Students should keep their vocabulary work as study materials for the unit test.

Reading Assignment Sheet   You need to fill in the reading assignment sheet to let students know by when their reading has to be completed. You can either write the assignment sheet up on a side blackboard or bulletin board and leave it there for students to see each day, or you can photocopy schedules for each student to have. In either case, you should advise students to become very familiar with the reading assignments so they know what is expected of them.

Extra Activities Center   The Unit Resource Materials portion of this LitPlan contains suggestions for an extra library of related books and articles in your classroom as well as crossword and word search puzzles. Make an extra activities center in your room where you will keep these materials for students to use. (Bring the books and articles in from the library and keep several copies of the puzzles on hand.) Explain to students that these materials are available for students to use when they finish reading assignments or other class work early.

Nonfiction Assignment Sheet   Explain to students that they each are to read at least one non-fiction piece from the in-class library at some time during the unit. Students will fill out a nonfiction assignment sheet after completing the reading to help you (the teacher) evaluate their reading experiences and to help the students think about and evaluate their own reading experiences.

Books   Each school has its own rules and regulations regarding student use of school books. Advise students of the procedures that are normal for your school.

Activity #4
Have students look at and read through the study questions for the Prologue and Parodos. This can be done silently or orally.

Activity #5
Do the first vocabulary worksheet (for Prologue and Parodos) orally, together as a class, to show students how the vocabulary worksheets should be done prior to each reading assignment.

Activity #6
Assign roles for the Prologue and Parodos of *Oedipus Rex* to students. Those students, when doing their homework, should prepare to read the parts aloud in class in lesson 3. Encourage them to PERFORM, not just read the words.
All students should read the Prologue and Parodos prior to the next class period. If time remains in class, students may begin reading silently.

LESSON TWO

Objectives
1. To review the main events and ideas from the Prologue and Parodos
2. To discuss a brief history of Greek Theatre
3. To enhance research skills through the use of the library/media center
4. To demonstrate reading comprehension skills through completion of a non-fiction assignment about the life of the playwright, Sophocles
5. To preview the vocabulary worksheet and study guide questions for Scene1 and Ode 1
6. To read Scene 1 and Ode 1

Activity #1

Give students a few minutes to formulate answers for the study guide questions for the Prologue and the Parodos, and then discuss the answers to the questions in detail. Write the answers on the board or overhead transparency so students can have the correct answers for study purposes.

Note: It is a good practice in public speaking and leadership skills for individual students to take charge of leading the discussions of the study questions. Perhaps a different student could go to the front of the class and lead the discussion each day that the study questions are discussed during this unit. Of course, the teacher should guide the discussion when appropriate and be sure to fill in any gaps the students leave.

Activity #2

Discuss each of the following and their importance to Greek Theatre:

- **Dionysus:** the Greek god of wine, fertility and rebirth. The theatrical performances were originally religious ceremonies in honor of Dionysus.
- **the Dionysia:** the name of the annual festival held in honor of Dionysus
- **Thespis:** This man is accredited as the "inventor of tragedy," and he was the first prize winner at the Great Dionysia in 534 BC. He was an important innovator for the theatre because he introduced the concept of the independent actor (that's why actors are called "thespians") as opposed to the choir, as well as the use of masks, make up and costumes so that the actor could play several roles.
- **Aeschylus:** He is accredited as the man who first increased the number of the actors from one (a la Thespis) to two, and he is accredited with reducing the role of the chorus, putting emphasis on dialogue (conversation between two or more characters). Sophocles is accredited with going one step further by introducing three or more actors on the stage.
- **Satyr:** The Satyr Play, commonly confused with "satire", had to be mastered by tragedians and was comprised of the following elements:

- o Chorus-half-man, half-beast - satyrs, companions of Dionysus
- o sometimes the story is connected with the tragedy it accompanies, but not usually
- o burlesque of mythology - ridiculing gods or heroes
- o structure similar to tragedy
- o everyday and colloquial language
- o shorter after-pieces to tragedies
- **The Use of Masks**: The chorus usually wore similar masks so as to unify them as a "group," but actors wore them to distinguish between various characters. Since all Greek actors were men, it was necessary to wear masks in order to portray female characters. On Day Eleven of this unit, students will be creating their own masks that they may wear when performing the odes they will be composing on Day Ten.

Activity #3

Give each student a non-fiction assignment sheet. Students will use the library/media center to find articles about the life of the playwright Sophocles in order to complete the assignment sheet. In addition to the questions on the sheet itself, students must provide information surrounding at least *three* other contributions that Sophocles made to the Greek society outside of his contributions to the theatre.

Activity #4

Tell students to preview the study questions, do the vocabulary worksheet, and read Scene 1 and Ode 1 prior to the next class meeting.

Activity #5

Assign roles for Scene 1 and Ode 1 of *Oedipus Rex* to students. Those students, when doing their homework, should prepare to read the parts aloud in class in lesson 3. Encourage them to PERFORM, not just read the words.

All students should read Scene 1 and Ode 1 prior to the next class period. If time remains in class, students may begin reading silently.

NONFICTION ASSIGNMENT SHEET
Oedipus Rex
(To be completed after reading the required nonfiction article/s)

Name _____ Date _____

Title of Nonfiction Read _____

Written by _____ Publication Date _____

I. Factual Summary: Write a short summary of the piece you read.

II. Vocabulary
1. With which vocabulary words in the piece did you encounter some degree of difficulty?

2. How did you resolve your lack of understanding with these words?

III. Interpretation: What was the main point the author wanted you to get from reading his work?

IV. Criticism
1. With which points of the piece did you agree or find easy to accept? Why?

2. With which points of the piece did you disagree or find difficult to believe? Why?

V. Personal Response: What do you think about this piece? <u>OR</u> How does this piece influence your ideas?

VI: Extended Response: On the back of this sheet, discuss three other contributions that Sophocles made to the Greek society.

LESSON THREE

Objective:
1. To review the main events and ideas from Scene 1 and Ode 1
2. To improve oral reading skills through performing the play
3. To practice note taking/critiquing skills while listening to other's presentations
4. To preview the vocabulary worksheet and study guide questions for Scene2 and Ode 2
5. To read Scene 2 and Ode 2

Activity #1
    Give students a few minutes to formulate answers for the study guide questions for the Scene 1 and Ode 1, and then discuss the answers to the questions in detail. Write the answers on the board or overhead transparency so students can have the correct answers for study purposes

Activity #2
    If you have not yet completed an oral reading evaluation for your students this period, this would be a good opportunity to do so.
    Arrange desks into a "U" shape (to allow for the illusion of an "amphitheatre"). Students at their desks watch as the Prologue, Parodos, Scene 1, and Ode 1 are acted out by the students assigned to each part. Each "audience member" is assigned a particular character to watch and critique. They are to make notes of performance skills and offer written feedback (three positive comments and two comments on how the performer could improve his/her performances in the future). Also, each student is to identify three specific traits that their assigned character seems to exhibit through his/her speeches. Since the "audience" members will be reading the Ode as the Chorus, the feedback sheets should be limited to the Prologue, Parodos, and Scene I. Be sure that those who formulate the chorus (all of the students who are NOT cast as specific characters will be in the chorus for the Ode) are divided into the strophe and the antistrophe, and that they move across the "stage" accordingly.
    Stop at the end of each section to discuss the action and the events occurring. Selecting one character at a time, discuss the character traits identified by the "audience members." Be sure that each trait can be backed up with textual support.
    Continue until the end of the Ode I.

Activity #3
    Tell students to preview the study questions, do the vocabulary worksheet, and read Scene 2 and Ode 2 prior to the next class meeting.

Activity #4
    Assign roles for Scene 2 and Ode 2 of *Oedipus Rex* to students. Those students, when doing their homework, should prepare to read the parts aloud in class in Lesson Five. Encourage them to PERFORM, not just read the words.
All students should read Scene 2 and Ode 2 prior to the next class period. If time remains in class, students may begin reading silently.

ORAL READING EVALUATION
Oedipus Rex

Name _____ Class _____ Date _____

SKILL	EXCELLENT	GOOD	AVERAGE	FAIR	POOR
<u>FLUENCY</u>	5	4	3	2	1
<u>CLARITY</u>	5	4	3	2	1
<u>AUDIBILITY</u>	5	4	3	2	1
<u>PRONUNCIATION</u>	5	4	3	2	1
_____	5	4	3	2	1
_____	5	4	3	2	1
_____	5	4	3	2	1

Total Grade:

Comments:

PEER PERFORMANCE FEEDBACK SHEET
Oedipus Rex

Name of Critic: _____ Character: _____

Dear Fellow Thespian,

Thank you for your performance! I liked the way you:

1.

2.

3.

However, I would have liked to have seen the following included in your performance. Perhaps you could take these into consideration for future performances:

1.

2.

Based on what I heard from your character, I would say that he/she demonstrates the following traits (include textual reference):

1.

2.

3.

Further comments:

LESSON FOUR

Objectives

1. To review the main events and ideas from Scene 2 and Ode 2
2. To demonstrate understanding of the play through taking a quiz
3. To be introduced to the "ode" style of poetry through John Keats's "Ode to a Nightingale"
4. To preview the vocabulary worksheet and study questions for Scene 3 and Ode 3
5. To read Scene 3 and Ode 3

Activity #1

Give students a few minutes to formulate answers for the study guide questions for Scene 2 and Ode 2 and then discuss the answers to the questions in detail. Write the answers on the board or overhead transparency so students can have the correct answers for study purposes

Activity #2

Quiz - Distribute quizzes for the Prologue through Ode 1, and give students about 10 minutes to complete them.

Note: The quizzes may either be the short answer study guides or the multiple choice version. Have students exchange papers. Grade the quizzes as a class. Collect the papers for recording the grades. If you used the multiple choice version as a quiz, take a few minutes to discuss the answers for the short answer version if your students are using the short answer version for their study guides.

Activity #3

Pass out copies and read aloud "Ode to a Nightingale" by John Keats. Ask students to try to define what an *ode* is. (The definition of an ode is a poem praising and glorifying a person, place or thing. It is usually written in an elevated style and often expresses deep feeling. Also, a copy of Keats' poem is included in this LitPlan since it has gone into public domain).

What is Keats praising in his poem? Ask students to re-read the first two stanzas and identify as many uses of figurative language/poetic devices that they can find (imagery, symbolism, simile, metaphor, personification, allusion, etc). Go through the first two stanzas together as a class, and then break the class up into six groups. Assign each group one of the six remaining stanzas and have them repeat the process. Have the groups share their findings with the rest of the class and explain how each poetic device enhances the poem as a whole.

Activity #4

Tell students to preview the study questions, do the vocabulary worksheet, and read Scene 3 and Ode 3 prior to the next class meeting.

Activity #5

Assign roles for Scene 3 and Ode 3 of *Oedipus* to students. Those students, when doing their homework, should prepare to read the parts aloud in class in lesson 5. Encourage them to PERFORM, not just read the words. All students should read Scene 3 and Ode 3 prior to the next class period. If time remains in class, students may begin reading silently.

"Ode to a Nightingale" by John Keats (1795-1821)

My heart aches, and a drowsy numbness pains
My sense, as though of hemlock I had drunk,
Or emptied some dull opiate to the drains
One minute past, and Lethe-wards had sunk:
'Tis not through envy of thy happy lot,
But being too happy in thine happiness,--
That thou, light-winged Dryad of the trees
In some melodious plot
Of beechen green, and shadows numberless,
Singest of summer in full-throated ease.

O, for a draught of vintage! that hath been
Cool'd a long age in the deep-delved earth,
Tasting of Flora and the country green,
Dance, and Provençal song, and sunburnt mirth!
O for a beaker full of the warm South,
Full of the true, the blushful Hippocrene,
With beaded bubbles winking at the brim,
And purple-stained mouth;
That I might drink, and leave the world unseen,
And with thee fade away into the forest dim:

Fade far away, dissolve, and quite forget
What thou among the leaves hast never known,
The weariness, the fever, and the fret
Here, where men sit and hear each other groan;
Where palsy shakes a few, sad, last gray hairs,
Where youth grows pale, and spectre-thin, and dies;
Where but to think is to be full of sorrow
And leaden-eyed despairs,
Where Beauty cannot keep her lustrous eyes,
    Or new Love pine at them beyond to-morrow.

Away! away! for I will fly to thee,
Not charioted by Bacchus and his pards,
But on the viewless wings of Poesy,
Though the dull brain perplexes and retards:
Already with thee! tender is the night,
And haply the Queen-Moon is on her throne,
Cluster'd around by all her starry Fays;
But here there is no light,
Save what from heaven is with the breezes blown
Through verdurous glooms and winding mossy ways.

I cannot see what flowers are at my feet,
Nor what soft incense hangs upon the boughs,
But, in embalmed darkness, guess each sweet
Wherewith the seasonable month endows
The grass, the thicket, and the fruit-tree wild;
White hawthorn, and the pastoral eglantine;
Fast fading violets cover'd up in leaves;
And mid-May's eldest child,
The coming musk-rose, full of dewy wine,
The murmurous haunt of flies on summer eves.

Darkling I listen; and, for many a time
I have been half in love with easeful Death,
Call'd him soft names in many a mused rhyme,
To take into the air my quiet breath;
Now more than ever seems it rich to die,
To cease upon the midnight with no pain,
While thou art pouring forth thy soul abroad
In such an ecstasy!
Still wouldst thou sing, and I have ears in vain--
To thy high requiem become a sod.

Thou wast not born for death, immortal Bird!
No hungry generations tread thee down;
The voice I hear this passing night was heard
In ancient days by emperor and clown:
Perhaps the self-same song that found a path
Through the sad heart of Ruth, when, sick for home,
She stood in tears amid the alien corn;
The same that oft-times hath
Charm'd magic casements, opening on the foam
Of perilous seas, in faery lands forlorn.

Forlorn! the very word is like a bell
To toll me back from thee to my sole self!
Adieu! the fancy cannot cheat so well
As she is fam'd to do, deceiving elf.
Adieu! adieu! thy plaintive anthem fades
Past the near meadows, over the still stream,
Up the hill-side; and now 'tis buried deep
In the next valley-glades:
Was it a vision, or a waking dream?
Fled is that music:--Do I wake or sleep?

LESSON FIVE

Objectives
1. To review the main events and ideas from Scene 3 and Ode 3
2. To improve oral reading skills through performing the play
3. To practice note taking/critiquing skills while listening to other's presentations
4. To preview the vocabulary worksheet and study guide questions for Scene 4 and Ode 4
5. To read Scene 4 and Ode 4

Activity #1
    Give students a few minutes to formulate answers for the study guide questions for Scene 3 and Ode 3, and then discuss the answers to the questions in detail. Write the answers on the board or overhead transparency so students can have the correct answers for study purposes.

Activity #2
    See directions for oral performance from Day Three of this unit. Repeat the process using Scene 2/Ode 2 and Scene 3/Ode 3. Use the same forms for the Teacher and the Student Feedback.

Activity #3
    Tell students to preview the study questions, do the vocabulary worksheet, and read Scene 4 and Ode 4 prior to the next class meeting.

Activity #4
    Assign roles for Scene 4 and Ode 4 of *Oedipus Rex* to students. Those students, when doing their homework, should prepare to read the parts aloud in class in lesson 8. Encourage them to PERFORM, not just read the words.
    All students should read Scene 4 and Ode 4 prior to the next class period. If time remains in class, students may begin reading silently.

LESSON SIX

<u>Objectives</u>
1. To review the main events and ideas from Scene 4 and Ode 4
2. To work in cooperative groups to analyze Sophocles's use of characterization in his tragedy
3. To demonstrate understanding of the play through taking a quiz
4. To preview the vocabulary worksheet and study guide questions for the Exodos
5. To read the Exodos

<u>Activity #1</u>
Give students a few minutes to formulate answers for the study guide questions for Scene 4 and Ode 4, and then discuss the answers to the questions in detail. Write the answers on the board or overhead transparency so students can have the correct answers for study purposes.

<u>Activity #2</u>
Quiz - Distribute quizzes for Scene 2 through Ode 3, and give students about 10 minutes to complete them.
(Note: The quizzes may either be the short answer study guides or the multiple choice version.) Have students exchange papers. Grade the quizzes as a class. Collect the papers for recording the grades. (If you used the multiple choice version as a quiz, take a few minutes to discuss the answers for the short answer version if your students are using the short answer version for their study guides.)

<u>Activity #3</u>
Divide students into 6 groups for the following: Oedipus, Iocaste, Creon, Teiresias, the Choragos/Chorus, the Corinthian messenger
Each group will be given a large sheet of construction paper to be used to create a character poster. On each poster, the groups must provide the following:
- the name of the character
- a labeled picture of the character based on the physical description given in the text
- a list of at least three positive character traits with supporting evidence and corresponding scene and line numbers for each
- a list of at least three negative character traits with supporting evidence and corresponding scene and line numbers for each

NOTE: treat the chorus and the choragus as though they were individual characters, and use the odes to characterize them. As for physical description, use what you know about the Greek theatre to draw them.

<u>Activity #4</u>
After students finish their posters, each pair/group will get up in front of the class and share the information about its particular character. Those who are not presenting must take notes about the other characters. Remind students that they will all be responsible for being able to identify all of the characters on the unit test.

Activity #5
Tell students to preview the study questions, do the vocabulary worksheet, and read the Exodos prior to the next class meeting.

Activity #6
Assign roles for the Exodos of *Oedipus Rex* to students. Those students, when doing their homework, should prepare to read the parts aloud in class in lesson 8. Encourage them to PERFORM, not just read the words.
All students should read the Exodos prior to the next class period. If time remains in class, students may begin reading silently.

LESSON SEVEN

Objectives
1. To review the main events and ideas from the Exodos
2. To enhance research skills through a visit to the school's library/media center
3. To practice writing to inform

Activity #1
    Give students a few minutes to formulate answers for the study guide questions for the Exodos, and then discuss the answers to the questions in detail. Write the answers on the board or overhead transparency so students can have the correct answers for study purposes.

Activity #2
    Distribute Writing Assignment #1 (informative piece) about the Aristotle's *Poetics* and the six elements of tragedy. Take students to the library/media center where they can begin their research in preparation for this assignment.
    The six elements are (for your information):
    I. plot – how the action is arranged
        A. *tragedy*: a play with a serious theme that usually ends unhappily for the main character set in motion by some tragic flaw in his/her personality (harmartia).
        B. *hubris*: arrogance demonstrated by a character as a result of his/her pride or passion
        C. *foreshadowing*: clues as to what will probably happen later in the play
        D. *climax*: the highest point of emotional tension or the turning point of the plot
        E. *catharsis*: the purification of a character's emotions and/or the relief of emotional tension
        F. *denouement:* the resolution of the main conflict (not usually a happy outcome for the main character)
    II. characters – the people in the play
    III. theme – the main idea or message as the central focus
    IV. language/diction – the words spoken or sung by the characters
    V. music – the odes sung by the chorus and choragus (in Greek tragedy)
    VI. spectacle – the scenes, props, costumes, masks… anything visual

WRITING ASSIGNMENT #1
Oedipus Rex
Informational Writing: Aristotle's *Poetics* and the six elements of tragedy

PROMPT
You are reading the Greek tragedy *Oedipus Rex* by Sophocles, and the class has been exploring Sophocles's influence in the Greek Theatre. However, Greek philosopher Aristotle also had an impact on Greek Theatre. Research Aristotle's *Poetics* and his six elements of a tragedy and then write a paper that connects Aristotle's elements of tragedy to Sophocles' *Oedipus Rex*.

PREWRITING
Research the required information at the library/media center. List Aristootle's 6 elements of a tragedy. Under each make notes about how they are demonstrated in Oedipus Rex. Use specific references to the text when possible. Jot down quotes and/or page numbers as quick reference points for when you write.

DRAFTING
Introduce your topic in the first paragraph, being sure to end with a thesis statement. Then write 6 body paragraphs, each describing one of Aristotle's elements of a tragedy and how it is a part of the structure of *Oedipus Rex*. Be sure to include embedded quotations from your research as support. Also, incorporate at least four vocabulary words from the unit into your essay.

PEER CONFERENCE/REVISING
When you finish the draft, ask another student to look at it. You may want to give the student your worksheets and articles so he/she can double check to see if you have included all the information you intended to include. After reading, he/she should tell you what is best about your essay, which parts were difficult to understand or follow, and ways in which your essay could be improved. Reread your essay considering your critic's comments and make the corrections you think are necessary.

PROOFREADING/EDITING
Do a final proofreading of your essay, double-checking your grammar, spelling, organization, and the clarity of your ideas.

WRITING EVALUATION FORM
Oedipus Rex

Name _____ Date _____

Grade _____

Circle One For Each Item:

Grammar:	correct	errors noted on paper
Spelling:	correct	errors noted on paper
Punctuation:	correct	errors noted on paper
Legibility:	excellent	good fair poor
_____	excellent	good fair poor
_____	excellent	good fair poor

Strengths:

Weaknesses:

Comments/Suggestions:

LESSON EIGHT

Objectives
1. To improve oral reading skills through performing the play
2. To practice note taking/critiquing skills while listening to other's presentations
3. To work independently on Writing Assignment

Activity #2
See directions for oral performance from Day Three of this unit. Repeat the process using Scene 4/Ode 4 and the Exodos. Use the same forms for the Teacher and the Student Feedback.

Activity #3
Allow students the opportunity to work on Writing Assignment #1 if you have time.

LESSON NINE

Objectives
1. To demonstrate understanding of the play through taking a quiz
2. To demonstrate the understanding of dramatic irony and apply to *Oedipus Rex*

Activity #1

Quiz - Distribute quizzes for Scene 4 through the Exodos, and give students about 10 minutes to complete them.
(Note: The quizzes may either be the short answer study guides or the multiple choice version.) Have students exchange papers. Grade the quizzes as a class. Collect the papers for recording the grades. (If you used the multiple choice version as a quiz, take a few minutes to discuss the answers for the short answer version if your students are using the short answer version for their study guides.)

Activity #2

Define the three types of irony (verbal irony, situational irony, dramatic irony) and ask students to give examples of each from real life, television, movies, or literature. Write their responses on the board under the proper heading (verbal, situational, or dramatic) and ask them to explain why the responses fit that particular type of irony.

Activity #3

Divide the class into 5 groups and assign each group one of the following speeches from *Oedipus Rex*. Each group is to read the speech and then look for evidence of irony.
1. Oedipus's monologue near the end of the Prologue
2. Oedipus's long monologue at the opening of Scene 1
3. Teiresias's monologue in Scene I (begin with "Listen to me. You mock my blindness, do you?")
4. Iocaste's monologue offering proof that soothsayer's lie in Scene 2
5. Oedipus's final speech in Scene 3

Thought Provoking Question: How does Dramatic Irony in each speech add to the tension of the play?

Have each group present its findings to the rest of the class.

LESSON TEN

Objectives
1. To review the use of figurative language in, as well as be able to define, an ode as a poetic form (review from Lesson Four)
2. To analyze the four odes in Sophocles's *Oedipus Rex* for the use of figurative language by the poet
3. To practice creative writing

Activity #1
Refer back to the exercise with "Ode to a Nightingale" by John Keats (Lesson Four) and review his use of poetic techniques.

Activity #2
Divide class into four groups, assign one of the odes from *Oedipus Rex* to each group and repeat the process used for Keats's ode. What is being praised/glorified in each? What poetic devices does Sophocles use in his odes, and how do they affect the poem as a whole? Again, students share their findings and encourage all to take notes that they can use to study for the unit test.

Activity #3
Pass out Writing Assignment #2, and have students begin creating their own odes that will be later presented to the class. Remember that an ode praises/glorifies something, and students must use at least four types of figurative language/poetic devices in their odes.

WRITING ASSIGNMENT #2
Oedipus Rex
Creative Expression: Writing an Ode

PROMPT
You are reading the Greek tragedy *Oedipus Rex* by Sophocles, and the class has been exploring Sophocles's use of the Poetic Ode at the end of each major scene. Review your notes about ode poetry in general, and then write your own ode about something that is important to you, imitating Sophocles's style in *Oedipus Rex*. Be sure to include both a Strophe and an Antistrophe.

PREWRITING
Choose one of the odes in Sophocles's *Oedipus Rex* that will be your model for the creation of your own ode. Examine each stanza and imitate its style in your glorification of whatever is important to you.

DRAFTING
Create the same number of stanzas, using both a Strophe and an Antistrophe, in your ode as in the model you selected from *Oedipus Rex*. Be sure to examine Sophocles's use of rhyme scheme and incorporate it into your own ode.

PEER CONFERENCE/REVISING
When you finish the draft, ask another student to look at it. You may want to give the student any notes you may have taken about Sophocles's ode so he/she can double check to see you have included all the stanzas/rhyme scheme you intended to include. After reading, he/she should tell you what is best about your poem, which parts were difficult to understand or follow, and ways in which your poem could be improved. Reread your poem considering your critic's comments and make the corrections you think are necessary.

PROOFREADING/EDITING
Do a final proofreading of your ode, double-checking your grammar, spelling, organization, and the clarity of your ideas. Memorize for performance day!

LESSON ELEVEN

<u>Objectives</u>
To create masks that reflect the creative writing assignment

<u>Activity #1</u>
Allow students to create the masks that will be needed for the performance of their odes. Mardi-Gras half-masks work well for this project, and they can be purchased cheaply on the Internet or you can get them at a craft store. You could also ask students in advance to purchase their own plain masks and then decorate them in class. Be sure to have on hand (students could also be asked to bring in contributions, or ask the Art department for any spare materials):

glue - beads
scissors - feathers
sequins - poster paint
glitter - ribbon
construction paper - any other materials that could be used!

The masks should contain symbolic representations of the odes they are in the process of writing. Students should make sure that they memorize their odes for their performances!

<u>Activity #2:</u>
Students may continue working on their odes.

LESSON TWELVE

Objective
   To review all of the vocabulary work done in this unit

Activity
   Choose one (or more) of the vocabulary review activities listed below and spend your class period as directed in the activity. Some of the materials for these review activities are located in the Vocabulary Resource Materials section in this LitPlan.

VOCABULARY REVIEW ACTIVITIES

1. Divide your class into two teams and have an old-fashioned spelling or definition bee.

2. Give each of your students (or students in groups of two, three or four) an *Oedipus Rex* Vocabulary Word Search Puzzle. The person (group) to find all of the vocabulary words in the puzzle first wins.

3. Give students an *Oedipus Rex* Vocabulary Word Search Puzzle without the word list. The person or group to find the most vocabulary words in the puzzle wins.

4. Use an *Oedipus Rex* Vocabulary Crossword Puzzle. Put the puzzle onto a transparency on the overhead projector (so everyone can see it), and do the puzzle together as a class.

5. Give students an *Oedipus Rex* Vocabulary Matching Worksheet to do.

6. Divide your class into two teams. Use *Oedipus Rex* vocabulary words with their letters jumbled as a word list. Student 1 from Team A faces off against Student 1 from Team B. You write the first jumbled word on the board. The first student (1A or 1B) to unscramble the word wins the chance for his/her team to score points. If 1A wins the jumble, go to student 2A and give him/her a definition. He/she must give you the correct spelling of the vocabulary word which fits that definition. If he/she does, Team A scores a point, and you give student 3A a definition for which you expect a correctly spelled matching vocabulary word. Continue giving Team A definitions until some team member makes an incorrect response. An incorrect response sends the game back to the jumbled-word face off, this time with students 2A and 2B. Instead of repeating giving definitions to the first few students of each team, continue with the student after the one who gave the last incorrect response on the team. For example, if Team B wins the jumbled-word face-off, and student 5B gave the last incorrect answer for Team B, you would start this round of definition questions with student 6B, and so on. The team with the most points wins!

7. Have students write a story in which they correctly use as many vocabulary words as possible. Have students read their compositions orally! Post the most original compositions on your bulletin board!

8.. Play *I Have, Who Has?* *NOTE This requires preparation in advance. On 3x5 cards, write a vocabulary word on one side and a definition to another word on the other side of the card. Once you have completed a set, pass that cards out randomly, keeping one for yourself. You will start the game by saying, "Who Has…" and reading the definition on the card. The student who has the word on his/her card that matches the definition shouts, "I Have…" and reads the word. He/She then turns over the card and says "Who Has…" and play continues until the all the words/cards have been gone through.

LESSON THIRTEEN

Objectives
    To discuss the play on a deeper, more critical level

Activity
    Choose the questions from the Extra Discussion Questions/Writing Assignments which seem most appropriate for your students. A class discussion of these questions is most effective if students have been given the opportunity to formulate answers to the questions prior to the discussion. To this end, you may either have all the students formulate answers to all the questions, divide your class into groups and assign one or more questions to each group, or you could assign one question to each student in your class. The option you choose will make a difference in the amount of class time needed for this activity.

    NOTE: The use of graphic organizers may be helpful to students in preparing their answers. Encourage them to use any diagrams or graphics that they feel are necessary.

EXTRA DISCUSSION QUESTIONS/WRITING ASSIGNMENTS – *Oedipus Rex*

Interpretation
1. In the Prologue, the Priest describes specific events that plague the city of Thebes. What are these events? Explain how each event is linked to the central conflict of the play (Oedipus has unknowingly killed his father and married his mother).
2. What is your initial reaction to Oedipus' character based on his interaction with the Priest in the Prologue? His interaction with Teiresias? List his positive and negative traits, using textual support as evidence.
3. Fully explain why Teiresias does not wish to tell what he knows is true.
4. Examine the logic that Creon uses when Oedipus accuses him of plotting against the King. Are his reasons logical? Explain why or why not.
5. At what point does Iocaste realize the truth? Give evidence from the text as support.
6. What motivates Oedipus to continue on his quest for the truth despite all warnings to the contrary? What does this say about his character?
7. Where is the climax of this play? Support your choice.
8. Look at Creon's last words to Oedipus. In comparison to his actions in the Exodos, do his words seem exceptionally cruel? Explain your position.

Critical
1. Which plays a greater role in this play: fate or free will? Pay attention to the fact that each who was told the prophecy tried to avoid his/her fate. Then again, Oedipus could have stopped his search if he wanted to. Support your decision with evidence from the text.
2. Sophocles' uses plant symbolism several times in the tragedy. Examine each reference below, and use a Dictionary of Symbolism (can be found on the internet) to find the meaning of each. Why is each symbol appropriate for the line?
    a. "It could not be otherwise: he is crowned with *bay*,/The chaplet is thick with berries."
    b. "It could not be otherwise: he is crowned with bay,/The chaplet is thick with *berries*."
    c. "Come, then, my children: leave the altar steps,/Lift up your *olive boughs*."
3. Discuss the role of the Chorus in this tragedy. What is its function? What does the Chorus glorify/honor in each of the odes?
4. Discuss the playwright's use of dramatic irony throughout the tragedy.
5. Examine Iocaste's entrance in Scene II. How are her words to her husband like those of a scolding mother? Explain the irony of her lines.
6. What seems to be the role/value of soothsayers in Greek society? How does Teiresias fulfill that role?
7. Why is it particularly ironic that Teiresias, the prophet, is blind?
8. How does the fact that Oedipus refuses to let go of his quest for the truth affect the outcome of this play? What seems to be Sophocles' message?
9. Define "tragic hero". Does Oedipus fit this definition? Why or why not?

10. For each of the following characters, select an object and explain how that object could be used to symbolize that person's particular character traits:
    - Oedipus
    - Iocaste
    - Creon
    - Teiresias
11. Sophocles alludes to several Greek Gods/Goddesses throughout the play. Identify each and determine why each allusion is appropriate for this tragedy:
    - Phoibos Apollo
    - Artemis
    - the Furies
    - Hermes
    - the Muses
    - Pallas Athene
    - Zeus
    - Pan
    - Dionysos

Critical/Personal Response
1. Research the condition that psychiatrist Sigmund Freud called The Oedipus Complex. Tell what Freud meant by the complex, and relate it to the tragedy *Oedipus Rex*.
2. Teiresias claims that he has held his tongue regarding the truth of Oedipus' identity because he thought it was best to keep the truth hidden. Do you agree with his motives? Think of examples of others who have kept quiet about something/someone because they thought it was for the best.
3. Oscar Wilde once said, "The truth is rarely pure and never simple." How can that statement be reflected in *Oedipus Rex*?
4. Suppose King Oedipus had taken Iocaste's advice and given up on his quest for the truth. How might the play have had a different ending?
5. Suppose Oedipus had accepted the Crown of Corinth and ruled two countries simultaneously. What different direction might the play have taken?
6. Make of list of movies that could fit into the category of a tragedy. What elements are present in these movies that make them fit into this genre?

Personal Response
1. Is it always important to tell the truth? Are there ever instances where a lie could be for the greater good? Explain why or why not, and give examples to support your answer.
2. If you were told that something horrible was about to happen, how would you react? What would it take for you to believe this person?
3. Are you intrigued about the story of Oedipus and the Sphinx that seems to run in the background of this play? Do you intend to read about it? Why or why not?
4. How do you feel about the character of Oedipus? Do you feel sorry for him? Or did he get what he deserved? Explain.
5. If you were going to stage a production of *Oedipus Rex*, how might you go about staging the blinding scene? What stage effects would you use that might not have been available in Sophocles' day?
6. Pretend you are going to cast a film version of Oedipus Rex. What actors would you choose to portray the various characters and why?

LESSON FOURTEEN

Objectives
    To practice writing to persuade

Activity #1
    Distribute the writing assignment #3 to each student and discuss the directions in detail. Give students the remaining time to write the essay in class.

Activity #2
    In the event students finish early, they may work on more of the Extra Discussion Questions or work independently editing their odes.

WRITING ASSIGNMENT #3 – *Oedipus Rex*
Persuasive: Determining Fault

PROMPT
You have finished reading the Greek tragedy *Oedipus Rex* by Sophocles, and the class has been exploring the conflicts introduced in the play. Based on the outcome, who seems to be most at fault? Apollo? Oedipus? Iocaste? Or was it fate?

PREWRITING
Decide which of the characters listed above is most at fault for the outcome of the play. Create a list of reasons, with textual evidence, to support your decision.

DRAFTING
Introduce your topic in the first paragraph, being sure to end with a thesis statement. Your thesis statement should include who you believe is the most responsible. In your body paragraphs, make sure that you begin by discussing the situation surrounding Oedipus. Further body paragraphs should give several reasons why you believe the person/fate mentioned in your thesis statement is most responsible for the tragedy. Also, be sure to examine why the others are NOT as much at fault for the outcome. Incorporate at least four vocabulary words from the unit into your essay. End the conclusion by challenging your reader in some way.

PEER CONFERENCE/REVISING
When you finish the draft, ask another student to look at it. You may want to give the student your pre-writing notes and scenario so he/she can double check to see you have included all the information you intended to include. After reading, he/she should tell you what is best about your essay, which parts were difficult to understand or follow, and ways in which your essay could be improved. Reread your essay considering your critic's comments and make the corrections you think are necessary. You will be completing a peer editing form the next class.

PROOFREADING/EDITING
Do a final proofreading of your essay, double-checking your grammar, spelling, organization, and the clarity of your ideas.

LESSON FIFTEEN

<u>Objective</u>
1. To demonstrate their ability to assess another's writing thorough a peer editing exercise
2. To demonstrate their ability to accept constructive criticism and make changes in their writing when necessary

<u>Activity #1</u>
Put students in pairs for peer editing and give each student a peer evaluation form. Students will exchange their persuasive essays written in class the day before and make comments regarding content, language use, and conventions (under "Editor"). Students will return the essays to the writer and then they respond to their peer's comments about their own writing on the editing sheet (under "Writer"). After thanking his/her peer for their comments, the writer will revise and rewrite the essay to turn in for a grade.

<u>Activity #2</u>
Once students have edited and revised their writing and turned the essays in to be graded, they may work on finishing their projects for the upcoming presentations.

NOTE: You should collect the completed odes for photocopying. These copies will be distributed when the students perform for their peers.

Editor's Name _____ Date _____

Writer's Name
_____ Assignment _____

Peer Editing for Writing Assignments

A. Was the writer's position clearly stated?

If your answer is "yes," be sure to tell the writer what he/she did that you especially liked. If your answer is "no," tell the writer what he/she could have included in order to write a better essay.

Editor: _____

_____

_____

Writer: _____

_____

_____

B. Did he/she provide enough details to support his/her position?

If your answer is "yes," be sure to tell the writer what you especially liked about his/her response. If your Answer is "no," you must tell the writer how he/she could improve his/her response (adding specific details that were missed, connecting to position better, or adding embedded quotations).

Editor: _____

_____

_____

Writer: _____

_____

C. Identify sentence type
Be sure to know the difference between simple, simple with compound subject, simple with compound predicate, compound, complex, and compound-complex. Using the first body paragraph, correctly identify each sentence type. If there is sufficient sentence structure variety, tell the writer what he/she did well. If not, explain what he/she could have done differently.

Sentence 1: _____   *Sentence 5:* _____

Sentence 2: _____   *Sentence 6:* _____

Sentence 3: _____   *Sentence 7:* _____

Sentence 4: _____   *Sentence 8:* _____

Editor: _____
_____

Writer: _____
_____

D. Address the Focus Correction Areas
Did the writer follow the specifics of the essay such as (address each individually):

Organization:
Editor: _____

Writer: _____

Use of vocabulary words as directed:
Editor: _____

Writer: _____

Cite play when referring to characters in *Oedipus Rex*:
Editor: _____

Writer: _____

E. Check for errors in grammar, spelling, punctuation, etc.

Editor: _____

Writer: _____

LESSONS SIXTEEN and SEVENTEEN

Objectives
1. To practice public speaking skills through the presentations of their odes
2. To demonstrate their knowledge of the composition of an ode through their presentations

Activity #1

Distribute copies of the Peer Critique Form (one per student) as well as copies of each student's ode as he/she comes forward to recite. Assign each student a "personal critic" who will evaluate the ode as it is being performed (this is where the evaluation sheet will come into play). Each student should have the opportunity to evaluate a peer's presentation and provide feedback for him/her. The teacher, of course, will be evaluating as well. A presentation evaluation sheet has been provided for your convenience.

As each student comes forward to perform his/her memorized ode, the student should be wearing his/her mask that he/she created. Ask him/her to explain the mask when he/she has finished reciting the ode.

Activity #2

If there is any remaining time, the teacher can provide further vocabulary review materials or any of the other review materials in preparation for the unit test.

NOTE: Allow for two days for presentations of the odes. If you have any extra time, use it to review for the unit test or to review vocabulary.

Presentation Evaluation Sheet (Teacher Form)

Each of the following will be graded on a scale of 1-5, with 1 being the lowest; each is worth 20% of the overall grade.

- Part I: student's use of the preparation time in class (this has been monitored during in-class work)
- Part II: student's performance (how well he/she has memorized the piece, as well as the student's vocal performance: diction, rate, volume, vocal inflection, etc.)
- Part III: student's work fits the correct format of an ode based on the classroom study of odes
- Part IV: student is clear about what he/she is honoring/glorifying through the ode
- Part V: student's mask reflects his/her ode

Title of Ode: _____

Author: _____

Part I: _____

Part II: _____

Part III: _____

Part IV: _____

Part V: _____

Total Score: _____

PEER CRITIQUE FORM - Odes

Critic's Name: _____ Poet's name: _____

For each of the following, give a rating of 1-5, where 1 = poor and 5 = outstanding. Be sure to comment on your decision and tell the poet WHY you rated him/her so. Remember, "Good Job!" does not convey what it was he/she did that was so good! Be as constructive as possible!

I. Identify what is being glorified/honored. How well does the ode stay on topic? _____
Comment:

II. How well does the poet express the emotions that reflect the mood of the ode? _____
Comment:

III: How well does the poet use facial expressions or hand gestures to reflect the mood of the ode? _____
Comment:

IV: How well could you understand what the poet was saying (diction, volume, rate)? _____
Comment:

V: How well does the poet's mask reflect the ode? _____
Comment:

Thank you for sharing your ode with the class! I really liked that way you:

However, I really would have liked:

LESSON EIGHTEEN

Objective
　　　　To review the main ideas and events in *Oedipus Rex*

Activity #1
　　　　Choose one of the following review games/activities and spend your class time as directed there.

REVIEW GAMES/ACTIVITIES – *Oedipus Rex*

1. Ask the class to make up a unit test for *Oedipus Rex*. The test should have 4 sections: matching, true/false, short answer, and essay. Students may use 1/2 period to make the test and then swap papers and use the other 1/2 class period to take a test a classmate has devised. (open book) You may want to use the unit test included in this packet or take questions from the students' unit tests to formulate your own test.

2. Take 1/2 period for students to make up true and false questions (including the answers). Collect the papers and divide the class into two teams. Draw a big tic-tac-toe board on the chalk board. Make one team X and one team O. Ask questions to each side, giving each student one turn. If the question is answered correctly, that students' team's letter (X or O) is placed in the box. If the answer is incorrect, no letter is placed in the box. The object is to get three in a row like tic-tac-toe. You may want to keep track of the number of games won for each team.

3. Take 1/2 period for students to make up questions (true/false and short answer). Collect the questions. Divide the class into two teams. You'll alternate asking questions to individual members of teams A & B (like in a spelling bee). The question keeps going from A to B until it is correctly answered, then a new question is asked. A correct answer does not allow the team to get another question. Correct answers are +2 points; incorrect answers are -1 point.

4. Have students pair up and quiz each other from their study guides and class notes.

5. Give students an *Oedipus Rex* crossword puzzle to complete.

6. Divide your class into two teams. Use *Oedipus Rex* crossword words with their letters jumbled as a word list. Student 1 from Team A faces off against Student 1 from Team B. You write the first jumbled word on the board. The first student (1A or 1B) to unscramble the word wins the chance for his/her team to score points. If 1A wins the jumble, go to student 2A and give him/her a clue. He/she must give you the correct word which matches that clue. If he/she does, Team A scores a point, and you give student 3A a clue for which you expect another correct response. Continue giving Team A clues until some team member makes an incorrect response. An incorrect response sends the game back to the jumbled-word face off, this time with students 2A and 2B. Instead of repeating giving clues to the first few students of each team, continue with the student after the one who gave the last incorrect response on the team. For example, if Team B wins the jumbled-word face-off, and student 5B gave the last incorrect answer for Team B, you would start this round of clue questions with student 6B, and so on. The team with the most points wins!

7. Play *What's My Line?*. This is similar to the old television show. Students assume the roles of different characters from the tragedy. One student gives clues to the class, or to a panel of contestants.

The contestants try to guess the identity of the guest. Students may enjoy assisting you in creating rules and procedures for the game.

8. Play *Jeopardy*. Divide the class into two groups. Assign each group a category or scene from the play and have them devise answers for that category. Play the game according to the television show procedures.

9. Play *Drawing in the Details*. This is similar to Pictionary. Divide students into teams. A student from one team draws a scene from the tragedy. (You may want to specify the scene or ode.) Drawings should be kept simple, to keep the pace lively. Students in the opposing team locate the scene in their books and read it aloud. If they are incorrect, the illustrator's team has a chance to guess. Involve students in setting up a scoring system and any other necessary rules.

10. Play *I Have, Who Has?* *NOTE This requires preparation in advance. On 3x5 cards, write a clue word on one side and a clue/definition/question to another clue word on the other side of the card. Once you have completed a set, pass that cards out randomly, keeping one for yourself. You will start the game by saying, "Who Has…" and reading the definition/question on the card. The student who has the answer on his/her card that matches the definition/question shouts, "I Have…" and reads the answer. He/She then turns over the card and says "Who Has…" and play continues until the all the cards have been gone through.

LESSON NINETEEN – *Oedipus Rex*

Objective
To test the students understanding of the main ideas and themes in *Oedipus Rex*

Activity #1
Distribute the unit tests. Go over the instructions in detail and allow the students the entire class period to complete the exam.

NOTES ABOUT THE TESTS IN THIS UNIT:

There are 5 different unit tests which follow.

There are two short answer tests which are based primarily on facts from the tragedy. The answer key for short answer unit test 1 follows the student test. The answer key for short answer test 2 follows the student short answer unit test 2.

There is one advanced short answer unit test, and it is based on the extra discussion questions. Use the matching key for short answer unit test 2 to check the matching section of the advanced short answer unit test. There is no key for the short answer questions. The answers will be based on the discussions you have had during class.

There are two multiple choice unit tests. Following the two unit tests, you will find an answer sheet on which students should mark their answers. The same answer sheet should be used for both tests; however, students' answers will be different for each test. Following the students' answer sheet for the multiple choice tests you will find your two keys: one for multiple choice test 1 and one for multiple choice test 2.

The short answer tests have a vocabulary section. You should choose 10 of the vocabulary words from this unit, read them orally and have the students write them down. Then, either have students write a definition or use the words in sentences.

Use these words for the vocabulary section of the advanced short answer unit test:

augury	lustration	contagion	perquisites
compunction	malediction	suppliant	sirings
venerate	execrable	parricide	regicide

Activity #2
Collect all test papers and assigned books prior to the end of the class period.

UNIT TESTS

SHORT ANSWER UNIT TEST 1 – *Oedipus Rex*

I. Matching/Identify

_____ 1. Oedipus   A. songs that comment on the action of the play or its characters

_____ 2. Iocaste   B. the leader of the chorus

_____ 3. Polybos   C. terrorized the city of Thebes until Oedipus answered her riddle

_____ 4. Laios   D. a scene in a play

_____ 5. Creon   E. ill fated king who killed his father and married his mother

_____ 6. Antigone   F. a serious play in which the main character suffers from a flaw

_____ 7. Choragos   G. the last song of the play; usually contains a moral lesson

_____ 8. Teiresias   H. brother-in-law to Oedipus; accused of treason

_____ 9. Sphinx   I. one of the daughters of Oedipus

_____ 10. Chorus   J. an opening song as the chorus makes its entrance

_____ 11. Merope   K. was killed in an altercation where three roads met

_____ 12. Episode   L. the Queen of Corinth who raised Oedipus as her own

_____ 13. Apollo   M. Oedipus blames him for all of his troubles

_____ 14. Exodos   N. the movement of the chorus from left to right across the stage

_____ 15. Prologue   O. a blind prophet

_____ 16. Strophe   P. introduces the main characters in the beginning of a play

_____ 17. Antistrophe   Q. tried to kill her child to avoid a chilling prophecy

_____ 18. Parodos   R. group that sings and comments on the actions of the characters

_____ 19. Tragedy   S. raised a stranded infant Oedipus as his own child

_____ 20. Ode   T. the movement of the chorus from right to left across the stage

Oedipus Rex Short Answer Unit Test 1 Page2

II. Short Answer

1. What has been happening in Thebes that brings all members of the community to Oedipus's palace for answers?

2. Why had no one attempted to find out the truth about what had happened to Laois?

3. When Oedipus asks the prophet to reveal the name of the murderer, what is the prophet's response?

4. Who does Oedipus accuse of being behind a plot to destroy him?

5. What "proof" does Iocaste offer that prophets do not tell the truth?

Oedipus Rex Short Answer Unit Test 1 Page3

6. Why had Oedipus fled Corinth many years before?

7. What news does the messenger from Corinth bring to Thebes?

8. How did the old shepherd and the messenger from Corinth know each other?

9. What truth does Oedipus learn?

10. What happened to Iocaste? Oedipus?

Oedipus Rex Short Answer Unit Test 1 Page4

III. Essay

    Write a short essay about the life of Sophocles, including not only his contributions to the Greek theatre, but at least two other contributions he made in his society.

Oedipus Rex Short Answer Unit Test 1 Page 5

IV. Vocabulary

    Write down the vocabulary words. Go back later and write down the correct definition for each word.

1.

2.

3.

4.

5.

6.

7.

8.

9.

10.

SHORT ANSWER UNIT TEST 1 ANSWER KEY – *Oedipus Rex*

I. Matching/Identify

E 1. Oedipus	A.	songs that comment on the action of the play or its characters
Q 2. Iocaste	B.	the leader of the chorus
S 3. Polybos	C.	terrorized the city of Thebes until Oedipus answered her riddle
K 4. Laios	D.	a scene in a play
H 5. Creon	E.	ill fated king who killed his father and married his mother
I 6. Antigone	F.	a serious play in which the main character suffers from a flaw
B 7. Choragos	G.	the last song of the play; usually contains a moral lesson
O 8. Teiresias	H.	brother-in-law to Oedipus; accused of treason
C 9. Sphinx	I.	one of the daughters of Oedipus
R 10. Chorus	J.	an opening song as the chorus makes its entrance
L 11. Merope	K.	was killed in an altercation where three roads met
D 12. Episode	L.	the Queen of Corinth who raised Oedipus as her own
M 13. Apollo	M.	Oedipus blames him for all of his troubles
G 14. Exodos	N.	the movement of the chorus from left to right across the stage
P 15. Prologue	O.	a blind prophet
T 16. Strophe	P.	introduces the main characters in the beginning of a play
N 17. Antistrophe	Q.	tried to kill her child to avoid a chilling prophecy
J 18. Parodos	R.	group that sings and comments on the actions of the characters
F 19. Tragedy	S.	raised a stranded infant Oedipus as his own child
A 20. Ode	T.	the movement of the chorus from right to left across the stage

Oedipus Rex Short Answer Unit Test 1 Answer Key Page 2

II. Short Answer

1. What has been happening in Thebes that brings all members of the community to Oedipus's palace for answers?
   Plants and crops are dying, cattle/sheep are sick, unborn children are dying, and Thebes is becoming a wasteland.

2. Why had no one attempted to find out the truth about what had happened to Laois?
   The people of Thebes were too busy dealing with the Sphinx to investigate what had happened to Laios.

3. When Oedipus asks the prophet to reveal the name of the murderer, what is the prophet's response?
   He says that he has known all along, but he has made himself forget because he thinks it is better that no one knows.

4. Who does Oedipus accuse of being behind a plot to destroy him?
   Oedipus blames his brother-in-law Creon of plotting to destroy him.

5. What "proof" does Iocaste offer that prophets do not tell the truth?
   She says that her husband Laios was told that he'd be murdered by his own son. To avoid the prophecy, they'd left their infant to die in the mountains; therefore, Teiresias' accusations against Oedipus cannot possibly be true.

6. Why had Oedipus fled Corinth many years before?
   An oracle had told Oedipus that he was fated to kill his father and breed children with his own mother. He left Corinth to avoid this.

7. What news does the messenger from Corinth bring to Thebes?
   The King of Corinth, Polybos, is dead and Oedipus is to be crowned King of Corinth.

8. How did the old shepherd and the messenger from Corinth know each other?
   They had spent three seasons tending their flocks together on Mt. Kithairon.

9. What truth does Oedipus learn?
   He learns that he was the infant who grew up and killed King Laios (his father) at a crossroads after leaving Corinth, and that he unwittingly married his own mother after solving the Sphinx's riddle. She also bore him four children: two sons and two daughters.

10. What happened to Iocaste? Oedipus?
    Iocaste hanged herself in her apartment. Oedipus took the brooches from her dress and blinded himself with them. He is going to follow his own edict and go into self-exile.

Parts III and IV:
For the essay portion, answers will vary. The vocabulary section will depend on which words you select from the list.

SHORT ANSWER UNIT TEST 2 – *Oedipus Rex*

I. Matching/Identify

_____ 1. Oedipus   A. the Queen of Corinth who raised Oedipus as her own

_____ 2. Iocaste   B. a blind prophet

_____ 3. Polybos   C. the movement of the chorus from right to left across the stage

_____ 4. Laios   D. an opening song as the chorus makes its entrance

_____ 5. Creon   E. brother-in-law to Oedipus; accused of treason

_____ 6. Antigone   F. the movement of the chorus from left to right across the stage

_____ 7. Choragos   G. Oedipus blames him for all of his troubles

_____ 8. Teiresias   H. a scene in a play

_____ 9. Sphinx   I. ill fated king who killed his father and married his mother

_____ 10. Chorus   J. group that sings and comments on the actions of the characters

_____ 11. Merope   K. raised a stranded infant Oedipus as his own child

_____ 12. Episode   L. terrorized the city of Thebes until Oedipus answered her riddle

_____ 13. Apollo   M. the leader of the chorus

_____ 14. Exodos   N. tried to kill her child to avoid a chilling prophecy

_____ 15. Prologue   O. was killed in an altercation where three roads met

_____ 16. Strophe   P. the last song of the play; usually contains a moral lesson

_____ 17. Antistrophe   Q. a serious play in which the main character suffers from a flaw

_____ 18. Parodos   R. introduces the main characters in the beginning of a play

_____ 19. Tragedy   S. songs that comment on the action of the play or its characters

_____ 20. Ode   T. one of the daughters of Oedipus

Oedipus Rex Short Answer Unit Test 2 Page2

II. Short Answer

1. What deed had Oedipus accomplished that makes the people believe that he is "the man surest in mortal ways/And wisest in the ways of God"?

2. Who is Laios?

3. Who does the Choragos suggest could help Oedipus locate the whereabouts of the murderer?

4. What seems to be the attitude of the Chorus in Ode I toward the prophet's revelation?

5. What is Oedipus' reaction to hearing that Laios was killed in a place where three highways met?

Oedipus Rex Short Answer Unit Test 2 Page 3

6. What revelation does the Corinthian messenger make to Oedipus?

7. How does the shepherd react when the messenger states that King Oedipus was the baby the shepherd had given him?

8. Why had the infant been handed over to the shepherd to begin with?

9. What does Oedipus claim he will do now that the truth is known?

10. Who takes over as the ruler of Thebes?

Oedipus Rex Short Answer Unit Test 2 Page 4

III. Composition

    Define Dramatic Irony. How does Sophocles use dramatic irony to build the tension of *Oedipus Rex*? Give at least two examples from the play and explain the irony.

Oedipus Rex Short Answer Unit Test 2 Page5

IV. Vocabulary

    Write down the vocabulary words. Go back later and write down the correct definitions for the words.

1.

2.

3.

4.

5.

6.

7.

8.

9.

10.

ANSWER KEY: SHORT ANSWER UNIT TEST 2 – *Oedipus Rex*

I. Matching/Identify

I ____ 1. Oedipus	A.	the Queen of Corinth who raised Oedipus as her own
N ____ 2. Iocaste	B.	a blind prophet
K ____ 3. Polybos	C.	the movement of the chorus from right to left across the stage
O ____ 4. Laios	D.	an opening song as the chorus makes its entrance
E ____ 5. Creon	E.	brother-in-law to Oedipus; accused of treason
T ____ 6. Antigone	F.	the movement of the chorus from left to right across the stage
M ____ 7. Choragos	G.	Oedipus blames him for all of his troubles
B ____ 8. Teiresias	H.	a scene in a play
L ____ 9. Sphinx	I.	ill fated king who killed his father and married his mother
J ____ 10. Chorus	J.	group that sings and comments on the actions of the characters
A ____ 11. Merope	K.	raised a stranded infant Oedipus as his own child
H ____ 12. Episode	L.	terrorized the city of Thebes until Oedipus answered her riddle
G ____ 13. Apollo	M.	the leader of the chorus
P ____ 14. Exodos	N.	tried to kill her child to avoid a chilling prophecy
R ____ 15. Prologue	O.	was killed in an altercation where three roads met
C ____ 16. Strophe	P.	the last song of the play; usually contains a moral lesson
F ____ 17. Antistrophe	Q.	a serious play in which the main character suffers from a flaw
D ____ 18. Parodos	R.	introduces the main characters in the beginning of a play
Q ____ 19. Tragedy	S.	songs that comment on the action of the play or its characters
S ____ 20. Ode	T.	one of the daughters of Oedipus

Oedipus Rex Short Answer Unit Test 2 Answer Key   Page 2

II. Short Answer

1. What deed had Oedipus accomplished that makes the people believe that he is "the man surest in mortal ways/And wisest in the ways of God"?
    He saved Thebes from the Sphinx, a creature that had been killing the young men by correctly answering her riddle.

2. Who is Laios?
    Laios was the King of Thebes before Oedipus arrived. He'd left town on a pilgrimage and never returned.

3. Who does the Choragos suggest could help Oedipus locate the whereabouts of the murderer?
    The Choragos suggests the Oedipus send for the blind prophet Teiresias.

4. What seems to be the attitude of the Chorus in Ode I toward the prophet's revelation?
    The Chorus says that is cannot believe "these evil words" and that Teiresias is lying.

5. What is Oedipus's reaction to hearing that Laios was killed in a place where three highways met?
    He remembers an altercation he'd had many years ago at that same location.

6. What revelation does the Corinthian messenger make to Oedipus?
    The messenger tells Oedipus that Polybos, the King of Corinth has died. He also tells Oedipus that Polybos was not his biological father.

7. How does the shepherd react when the messenger states that King Oedipus was the baby the shepherd had given him?
    The old shepherd tells the Corinthian messenger to hold his tongue.

8. Why had the infant been handed over to the shepherd to begin with?
    A prophecy had claimed that the child would grow to kill his father and marry his mother. Laios and Iocaste were trying to avoid the fulfillment of the prophecy.

9. What does Oedipus claim he will do now that the truth is known?
    He is going to follow his own edict and go into self-exile.

10. Who takes over as the ruler of Thebes?
    Creon

ADVANCED SHORT ANSWER UNIT TEST – *Oedipus Rex*

I. Matching/Identify

____ 1. Oedipus   A. the Queen of Corinth who raised Oedipus as her own

____ 2. Iocaste   B. a blind prophet

____ 3. Polybos   C. the movement of the chorus from right to left across the stage

____ 4. Laios   D. an opening song as the chorus makes its entrance

____ 5. Creon   E. brother-in-law to Oedipus; accused of treason

____ 6. Antigone   F. the movement of the chorus from left to right across the stage

____ 7. Choragos   G. Oedipus blames him for all of his troubles

____ 8. Teiresias   H. a scene in a play

____ 9. Sphinx   I. ill fated king who killed his father and married his mother

____ 10. Chorus   J. group that sings and comments on the actions of the characters

____ 11. Merope   K. raised a stranded infant Oedipus as his own child

____ 12. Episode   L. terrorized the city of Thebes until Oedipus answered her riddle

____ 13. Apollo   M. the leader of the chorus

____ 14. Exodos   N. tried to kill her child to avoid a chilling prophecy

____ 15. Prologue   O. was killed in an altercation where three roads met

____ 16. Strophe   P. the last song of the play; usually contains a moral lesson

____ 17. Antistrophe   Q. a serious play in which the main character suffers from a flaw

____ 18. Parodos   R. introduces the main characters in the beginning of a play

____ 19. Tragedy   S. songs that comment on the action of the play or its characters

____ 20. Ode   T. one of the daughters of Oedipus

Oedipus Rex Advanced Short Answer Unit Test Page 2

II. Short Answer

1. In the Prologue, the Priest describes specific events that plague the city of Thebes. What are these events? Explain how each event is linked to the central conflict of the play (Oedipus has unknowingly killed his father and married his mother).

2. What is your initial reaction to Oedipus's character based on his interaction with the Priest in the Prologue? His interaction with Teiresias? List his positive and negative traits, using textual support as evidence.

3. Fully explain why Teiresias does not wish to tell what he knows is true.

4. At what point does Iocaste realize the truth? Give evidence from the text as support.

Oedipus Rex Advanced Short Answer Unit Test Page 3

5. What motivates Oedipus to continue on his quest for the truth despite all warnings to the contrary? What does this say about his character?

6. Why is it particularly ironic that Teiresias, the prophet, is blind?

7. How does the fact that Oedipus refuses to let go of his quest for the truth affect the outcome of this play? What seems to be Sophocles's message?

8. Define "tragic hero." Does Oedipus fit this definition? Why or why not?

Oedipus Rex Advanced Short Answer Unit Test Page 4

9. Oscar Wilde once said, "The truth is rarely pure and never simple." How can that statement be reflected in *Oedipus Rex*?

10. Discuss the playwright's use of dramatic irony throughout the tragedy.

Oedipus Rex Advanced Short Answer Unit Test Page5

III. Composition

Describe the six elements of tragedy as found in Aristotle's *Poetics*, and explain the function of each.

Oedipus Rex Advanced Short Answer Unit Test Page5

IV. Vocabulary
   A. Listen to the vocabulary words and write them here. Go back and write a definition for each.

1.

2.

3.

4.

5.

6.

7.

8.

9.

10.

11.

12.

For the following topic, include at least five of the vocabulary words in your response: Summarize the story of the Sphinx and explain Oedipus's response to her riddle.

MULTIPLE CHORUS UNIT TEST 1 – *Oedipus Rex*

I. Matching/Identify

____ 1. Oedipus A. songs that comment on the action of the play or its characters

____ 2. Iocaste B. the leader of the chorus

____ 3. Polybos C. terrorized the city of Thebes until Oedipus answered her riddle

____ 4. Laios D. a scene in a play

____ 5. Creon E. ill fated king who killed his father and married his mother

____ 6. Antigone F. a serious play in which the main character suffers from a flaw

____ 7. Choragos G. the last song of the play; usually contains a moral lesson

____ 8. Teiresias H. brother-in-law to Oedipus; accused of treason

____ 9. Sphinx I. one of the daughters of Oedipus

____ 10. Chorus J. an opening song as the chorus makes its entrance

____ 11. Merope K. was killed in an altercation where three roads met

____ 12. Episode L. the Queen of Corinth who raised Oedipus as her own

____ 13. Apollo M. Oedipus blames him for all of his troubles

____ 14. Exodos N. the movement of the chorus from left to right across the stage

____ 15. Prologue O. a blind prophet

____ 16. Strophe P. introduces the main characters in the beginning of a play

____ 17. Antistrophe Q. tried to kill her child to avoid a chilling prophecy

____ 18. Parodos R. group that sings and comments on the actions of the characters

____ 19. Tragedy S. raised a stranded infant Oedipus as his own child

____ 20. Ode T. the movement of the chorus from right to left across the stage

Oedipus Rex Multiple Choice Unit Test 1 Page 2

II. Multiple Choice

1. What has been happening in Thebes that brings all members of the community to Oedipus's palace for answers?
    A A terrible beast, a Sphinx, has been terrifying the city.
    B. A raging volcano has sent rivers of lava through the streets.
    C. A plague has descended upon the entire city; death and decay is everywhere.
    D. Gigantic swarms of locusts have descended upon the city.

2. Who is Creon?
    A. He is Oedipus's brother and second in command in Thebes.
    B. He is Oedipus's eldest son.
    C. He is Iocaste's, Oedipus's wife's brother.
    D. He is a priest at the temple of Delphi.

3. No one attempted to find out the truth about what had happened to Laois because:
    A. they were too busy trying to defeat the Sphinx that was terrifying Thebes.
    B. they thought they already knew the truth.
    C. Iocaste told the people that she was distraught enough without learning more.
    D. everyone who tried to learn the truth ended up dead.

4. What promise does Oedipus make to anyone who comes forward with information about Laios's murder?
    A. Oedipus will give a handsome reward of gold.
    B. He says that no harm will come to anyone who comes forward.
    C. He will give a formal pardon for the treason of withholding information.
    D. Oedipus makes no promises; he demands that anyone with information come forward.

5. When Oedipus asks the prophet to reveal the name of the murderer, what is the prophet's response?
    A. Although Teiresias knows the answer, it is better that no one else ever learns the truth.
    B. The king was never murdered at all; he is still alive in another land.
    C. He claims that Iocaste murdered her husband.
    D. He claims that he does not know because Apollo has kept the name from him.

6. Who does the prophet finally reveal as the murderer of King Laios?
    A. Iocaste
    B. Creon
    C. Teiresias
    D. Oedipus

Oedipus Rex Multiple Choice Unit Test 1 Page 3

7. What seems to be the attitude of the Chorus in Ode I toward the prophet's revelation?
    A. They are respectful because he is a wise man and should be listened to.
    B. They are angry because the prophet has spoken evil words and lies.
    C. They are afraid because they know the prophet speaks only the truth.
    D. They are vengeful because they believe that he is in on the death of King Laios

8. What is Creon's defense against the accusations against him?
    A. He claims that Laios's body was never returned to Thebes, so he could not have given Laios a proper burial.
    B. He says that he would never do anything to cause his sister, Iocaste, any pain.
    C. Why would he want the stress of being king when he already enjoys the same perks?
    D. He claims that Teiresias is a liar, and that his fate is his own; no evil awaits him.

9. What "proof" does Iocaste offer that prophets do not tell the truth?
    A. She had been told that she would marry her own son, but she'd killed the child.
    B. Her husband had been told that his own son would kill him, but he was killed by bandits at a crossroads.
    C. The rains never come exactly when they are predicted to.
    D. The gods create "fate" at their whim; the prophets cannot foresee the gods' intentions.

10. What is Oedipus's reaction to hearing that Laios was killed in a place where three highways met?
    A. He wants to go to the spot and search for clues to the murder.
    B. He remembers an altercation he once had in the some location.
    C. He is angry that a king would die in such an undignified manner.
    D. He wants to erect a monument at the place in Laios's memory.

11. Why had Oedipus fled Corinth many years before?
    A. An oracle told him that he would kill his father and marry his mother.
    B. He had killed a man.
    C. He was wrongly accused of treason by King Polybos.
    D. He wanted to go out and explore the world.

12. What news does the messenger from Corinth bring to Thebes?
    A. The King of Corinth is preparing to make war on Thebes.
    B. A warrant has been issued for Oedipus's arrest for treason.
    C. Oedipus's father, wishes for his son to pay a visit.
    D. The King of Corinth is dead, and Oedipus is to be crowned King.

Oedipus Rex Multiple Choice Unit Test 1 Page 4

13. How did Polybos die?
    A. He was killed by his son.
    B. He was murdered by his wife.
    C. He died of old age.
    D. His death is shrouded in mystery.

14. Specifically, what is Oedipus afraid of in Corinth?
    A. He is afraid that he will marry his mother and the two will bear children.
    B. He is afraid that he will be overcome by rage at being accused of treason.
    C. He is afraid that he will be executed for murder.
    D. He is afraid that he will be blamed for the death of the king.

15. How did Polybos come to raise Oedipus as his own son?
    A. Polybos is his father; it is natural that he would raise his son.
    B. Polybos found the abandoned infant Oedipus in the forest while out hunting.
    C. The messenger had been given an infant found in the mountains and he, in turn, gave the child to the king and queen.
    D. Although the illegitimate son of a servant girl, Polybos took the infant in when the girl died.

16. Who begs Oedipus to forget about finding the truth of his parentage?
    A. Creon
    B. Iocaste
    C. Teiresias
    D. the messenger from Corinth

17. How does the shepherd react when the messenger states that King Oedipus was the baby the shepherd had given him?
    A. He is surprised that the child had survived.
    B. He is repulsed by the fact that his king was of such a low birth.
    C. He tells the messenger to hold his tongue.
    D. He embraces Oedipus and weeps openly.

18. What truth does Oedipus learn?
    A. The shepherd is his true father.
    B. Iocaste has been unfaithful and his children are really the shepherd's children.
    C. The prophecy was right; he killed his father (Laios) and married his mother (Iocaste).
    D. Merope, his mother, had an affair with Laios, and Laios is his true father.

Oedipus Rex Multiple Choice Unit Test 1 Page 5

19. What happens to Iocaste?
    A. Oedipus strangles her.
    B. She hangs herself.
    C. Creon stabs her.
    D. She kills Teiresias because of his prophecies.

20. What does Oedipus claim he will do now that the truth is known?
    A. He will take his family and leave town.
    B. He will kill himself.
    C. He will exile himself just as he said he would do to the murderer of King Laios.
    D. He wants Creon to execute him.

Oedipus Rex Multiple Choice Unit Test 1 Page 6

III. Composition

1. What is your initial reaction to Oedipus's character based on his interaction with the Priest in the Prologue? His interaction with Teiresias? List his positive and negative traits, using textual support as evidence.

2. Discuss the playwright's use of dramatic irony throughout the tragedy.

3. At what point does Iocaste realize the truth? Give evidence from the text as support.

Oedipus Rex Multiple Choice Unit Test 1 Page 7

4. Why is it particularly ironic that Teiresias, the prophet, is blind?

5. How does the fact that Oedipus refuses to let go of his quest for the truth affect the outcome of this play? What seems to be Sophocles's message?

Oedipus Rex Multiple Choice Unit Test 1 Page 8

IV. Vocabulary - Match the correct definitions to the words.

____ 1. hearth   A. a group or clique within a larger group, party, government

____ 2. supplication   B. without rational basis

____ 3. faction   C. rude or impertinent behavior or speech

____ 4. edict   D. widespread and high repute; fame

____ 5. prudent   E. very unfortunate in condition or circumstances

____ 6. insolence   F. to take for granted, assume, or suppose

____ 7. decrepit   G. the floor of a fireplace, usually of stone, brick

____ 8. din   H. caused keen irritation or bitter resentment

____ 9. rankled   I. a person or thing that ruins or spoils

____ 10. abomination   J. weakened by old age; feeble

____ 11. groundless   K. any authoritative proclamation or command

____ 12. helmsman   L. forced or drove out

____ 13. wretched   M. a cloth or sheet in which a corpse is wrapped for burial

____ 14. expelled   N. to ask for humbly or earnestly, as by praying

____ 15. renown   O. moral weakness; liability to yield to temptation

____ 16. venerate   P. to regard or treat with reverence or respect

____ 17. shroud   Q. anything greatly disliked or abhorred

____ 18. bane   R. a person who steers a ship

____ 19. frailty   S. wise or judicious in practical affairs

____ 20. presume   T. a loud, disturbing noise

MULTIPLE CHOICE UNIT TEST 2 – *Oedipus Rex*

I. Matching

____ 1. Oedipus   A. the Queen of Corinth who raised Oedipus as her own

____ 2. Iocaste   B. a blind prophet

____ 3. Polybos   C. the movement of the chorus from right to left across the stage

____ 4. Laios   D. an opening song as the chorus makes its entrance

____ 5. Creon   E. brother-in-law to Oedipus; accused of treason

____ 6. Antigone   F. the movement of the chorus from left to right across the stage

____ 7. Choragos   G. Oedipus blames him for all of his troubles

____ 8. Teiresias   H. a scene in a play

____ 9. Sphinx   I. ill fated king who killed his father and married his mother

____ 10. Chorus   J. group that sings and comments on the actions of the characters

____ 11. Merope   K. raised a stranded infant Oedipus as his own child

____ 12. Episode   L. terrorized the city of Thebes until Oedipus answered her riddle

____ 13. Apollo   M. the leader of the chorus

____ 14. Exodos   N. tried to kill her child to avoid a chilling prophecy

____ 15. Prologue   O. was killed in an altercation where three roads met

____ 16. Strophe   P. the last song of the play; usually contains a moral lesson

____ 17. Antistrophe   Q. a serious play in which the main character suffers from a flaw

____ 18. Parodos   R. introduces the main characters in the beginning of a play

____ 19. Tragedy   S. songs that comment on the action of the play or its characters

____ 20. Ode   T. one of the daughters of Oedipus

Oedipus Rex Multiple Choice Unit Test 2 Page 2

II. Multiple Choice

1. What deed had Oedipus accomplished that makes the people believe that he is "the man surest in mortal ways/And wisest in the ways of God"?
    A. He'd solved the riddle of the Sphinx and it killed itself.
    B. He had defeated the Cretan Bull.
    C. He killed the Nemean Lion.
    D. He killed the Lernean Hydra, a nine headed monster.

2. What do the people of Thebes want Oedipus to do for them?
    A. They blame him for the problems and want him to leave town.
    B. They want him to rid Thebes of the problems and restore the city.
    C. They want him to make a sacrifice to Zeus to appease the gods.
    D. They want him to offer his youngest daughter to the fiery volcano.

3. What suggestion does Creon make when Oedipus asks about the message from the god, Apollo?
    A. Creon suggests that they make a sacrifice to Apollo as soon as possible.
    B. Creon suggests that Oedipus himself make a pilgrimage to Delphi.
    C. Creon suggests that they create stone levis to keep the lava out of the streets.
    D. Creon suggests that they talk privately somewhere about the god's message.

4. Who is Laios?
    A. He is Oedipus's eldest son.
    B. He is Creon's brother.
    C. He is Iocaste's first husband.
    D. He is a prophet.

5. The Chorus wants the gods to:
    A. destroy whatever enemy is bringing the plague upon Thebes.
    B. send them a hero to defend them.
    C. punish Oedipus for not following through on learning who murdered Laios.
    D. divert the molten lava away from Thebes.

6. Who does the Choragos suggest could help Oedipus locate the whereabouts of the murderer?
    A. Creon
    B. Teiresias
    C. Iocaste
    D. Apollo

Oedipus Rex Multiple Choice Unit Test 2 Page 3

7. What conclusion does Oedipus jump to when the prophet continually refuses to give specific information about the events surrounding the death of King Laios?
    A. Teiresias is a false prophet and has created prophecies for gold.
    B. The prophet is really King Laios in disguise.
    C. Teriesias must have been in on the plot to kill Laios.
    D. Teriesias is lying to cover up the fact that he has no prophetic powers.

8. Who does Oedipus accuse of being behind a plot to destroy him?
    A. Iocaste
    B. Teiresias
    C. Apollo
    D. Creon

9. Who does the Chorus say will follow the killer wherever he goes?
    A. the Fates
    B. the Furies
    C. Apollo
    D. Zeus

10. What convinces Oedipus to allow Creon to leave?
    A. The Choragos says that things are bad enough without the two of them fighting.
    B. He finally realizes that Creon is telling the truth.
    C. He did not have enough evidence against Creon, so he was forced to let him go.
    D. Iocaste begged for her brother's life and Oedipus relented.

11. What became of the only surviving member of the attack on King Laios's party?
    A. He hanged himself as soon as he returned.
    B. He became the leader of the new king's sentries.
    C. He begged Iocaste to send him as far from Thebes as possible.
    D. He was executed for failure to protect the king.

12. According to Ode II, what can be said about the hearts of mortals?
    A. They are weak in fear of the gods.
    B. They are strong in faith.
    C. They are loyal to their leaders.
    D. They no longer know Apollo, and have lost reverence for the gods.

13. How does Oedipus react to the Corinthian messenger's news?
    A. He is fearful of being charged with treason against the Corinthian crown.
    B. He is filled with relief.
    C. He prepares for war with Corinth.
    D. He prepares to visit his father.

Oedipus Rex Multiple Choice Unit Test 2 Page 4

14. Who does Oedipus claim to still fear in Corinth?
    A. He fears the family of the man he'd killed many years before.
    B. He fears Merope, the wife of Polybos.
    C. He fears the priest at the temple at Delphi.
    D. He fears the ghost of Polybos.

15. What revelation does the messenger make to Oedipus?
    A. King Polybos's murderer has already been caught.
    B. Oedipus was born to a servant of the King of Corinth, not to his mother Merope.
    C. The messenger is really King Laios who had been in hiding from Creon for years.
    D. Polybos was not Oedipus's natural father.

16. Upon what mountain had the infant Oedipus been found?
    A. Mt. Kithairon
    B. Mt. Sinai
    C. Mt. Olympus
    D. Mt. Everest

17. Who identified the old shepherd as the man who spared the infant Oedipus?
    A. Iocaste
    B. Creon
    C. Teiresias
    D. the Corinthian messenger

18. Why had the infant been handed over to the shepherd to begin with?
    A. He would grow to be more handsome than his own vain father.
    B. His poor parents could not afford to care for the child.
    C. It had been foretold that he would grow to kill his father and marry his mother.
    D. He was born with deformed feet and his parents did not want him.

19. What does Oedipus do after he held Iocaste in his arms?
    A. He slit her throat.
    B. He cries and tells her that he forgave her everything.
    C. He pushes her roughly aside in disgust.
    D. He takes the brooches from her gown and blinds himself.

20. Who takes over as the ruler of Thebes?
    A. Teiresias
    B. Polyneices, Oedipus's son
    C. Creon
    D. Eteocles, Oedipus's son

Oedipus Rex Multiple Choice Unit Test 2 Page 5

III. Composition

1. In the Prologue, the Priest describes specific events that plague the city of Thebes. What are these events? Explain how each event is linked to the central conflict of the play (Oedipus has unknowingly killed his father and married his mother).

2. Fully explain why Teiresias does not wish to tell what he knows is true.

3. What motivates Oedipus to continue on his quest for the truth despite all warnings to the contrary? What does this say about his character?

4. What seems to be the role/value of soothsayers in Greek society? How does Teiresias fulfill that role?

5. Define "tragic hero." Does Oedipus fit this definition? Why or why not?

Oedipus Rex Multiple Choice Unit Test 2 Page 6

IV. Vocabulary - Match the correct definitions to the words.

____ 1. liberator   A. fathering; siring

____ 2. compunction   B. person who professes to foretell events, fortune-teller

____ 3. besieger   C. an enemy who lays siege to your position

____ 4. begetting   D. broke up soil with a heavy framed tool with sharp teeth

____ 5. regicide   E. rude or impertinent behavior or speech

____ 6. pestilence   F. causing serious thoughts or a grave mood

____ 7. insolence   G. moving or acting in an aimless or vague manner

____ 8. brazen   H. a tomb, grave, or burial place

____ 9. parry   I. someone who releases people from captivity or bondage

____ 10. soothsayer   J. an empty space; emptiness

____ 11. maundering   K. the utterance of a curse

____ 12. malediction   L. being first in time; original

____ 13. sepulchre   M. shameless or impudent

____ 14. nymphs   N. one who is rejected or discarded

____ 15. solemn   O. any uneasiness or hesitation about the rightness of an action

____ 16. void   P. a period of watchful attention maintained at night

____ 17. harrowed   Q. female spirits in forests, water, and other places outdoors

____ 18. outcast   R. to turn aside; evade or dodge

____ 19. vigil   S. the killing of a king

____ 20. primal   T. something that is considered harmful, destructive, or evil

ANSWER SHEET MULTIPLE CHOICE UNIT TESTS
Oedipus Rex

	Matching	Mult. Choice	Vocabulary
1			
2			
3			
4			
5			
6			
7			
8			
9			
10			
11			
12			
13			
14			
15			
16			
17			
18			
19			
20			

ANSWER KEY MULTIPLE CHOICE UNIT TEST 1
Oedipus Rex

	Matching	Mult. Choice	Vocabulary
1	E	C	G
2	Q	C	N
3	S	A	A
4	K	B	K
5	H	A	S
6	I	D	C
7	B	B	J
8	O	C	T
9	C	B	H
10	R	B	Q
11	L	A	B
12	D	D	R
13	M	C	E
14	G	A	L
15	P	C	D
16	T	B	P
17	N	C	M
18	J	C	I
19	F	B	O
20	A	C	F

ANSWER KEY MULTIPLE CHOICE UNIT TEST 2
Oedipus Rex

	Matching	Mult. Choice	Vocabulary
1	I	A	I
2	N	B	O
3	K	D	C
4	O	C	A
5	E	A	S
6	T	B	T
7	M	C	E
8	B	D	M
9	L	B	R
10	J	A	B
11	A	C	G
12	H	D	K
13	G	B	H
14	P	B	Q
15	R	D	F
16	C	A	J
17	F	D	D
18	D	C	N
19	Q	D	P
20	S	C	L

UNIT RESOURCE MATERIALS

BULLETIN BOARD IDEAS – *Oedipus Rex*

1. Save one corner of the board for the best of students' *Oedipus Rex* writing assignments.

2. Take one of the word search puzzles from the extra activities packet and with a marker copy it over in a large size on the bulletin board. Write the clue words to find to one side. Invite students prior to and after class to find the words and circle them on the bulletin board.

3. Write several of the most significant quotations from the play onto the board on brightly colored paper.

4. Make a bulletin board listing the vocabulary words for this unit. As you complete sections of the play and discuss the vocabulary for each section, write the definitions on the bulletin board. (If your board is one students face frequently, it will help them learn the words.)

5. Create a bulletin board depicting the history of Greek Theatre

6. Devote an entire bulletin board to Sophocles and his life

7. Create "Ode to a Bulletin Board" and display student odes

8. Decorate a bulletin board with masks created by the students

9. Display the characterization posters completed by the students

10. Create an outline of the structure of a Greek tragedy

11. Create a bulletin board for the story of Oedipus and the Sphinx

12. Create a bulletin board devoted to the Sphinx and her riddles; display student riddles

13. Take pictures as the students perform (either from *Oedipus Rex* or reciting their odes) and display them on a bulletin board

14. Devote a bulletin board to Sigmund Freud and the study of the "Oedipus Complex"

15. Create a bulletin board devoted to soothsayers of today (such as Miss Cleo) with comments on fate vs. free will

EXTRA ACTIVITIES – *Oedipus Rex*

One of the difficulties in teaching a novel is that all students don't read at the same speed. One student who likes to read may take the book home and finish it in a day or two. Sometimes a few students finish the in-class assignments early. The problem, then, is finding suitable extra activities for students.

One thing that seems to help is to keep a little library in the classroom. For this unit on *Oedipus Rex*, you might check out from the school library *Oedipus at Colonus, Antigone,* and a collection of Greek myths. William Butler Yeats also did a translation of *Oedipus Rex* entitled *Oedipus the King*; this might make for some interesting comparisons or contrasts. Also, any stories or articles about Sophocles, Greek culture, Greek theatre (or theatre in general, for comparisons and/ or contrasts), or the society of Ancient Greece would also be of interest. Because this play is shrouded in mystery, perhaps some one-minute-mystery stories could be in the room and students could seek out the clues in the mysteries much like seeking out the clues in *Oedipus Rex*.

Other things you may keep on hand are puzzles. We have made some relating directly to *Oedipus Rex* for you. Feel free to duplicate them for your students to use.

Some students may like to draw. You might devise a contest or allow some extra-credit grade for students who draw characters or scenes from *Oedipus Rex*. Note, too, that if the students do not want to keep their drawings you may pick up some extra bulletin board materials this way. If you have a contest and you supply the prize (a CD or something like that perhaps), you could, possibly, make the drawing itself a non-returnable entry fee.

The pages which follow contain games, puzzles and worksheets. The keys, when appropriate, immediately follow the puzzle or worksheet. There are two main groups of activities: one group for the unit; that is, generally relating to *Oedipus Rex* text, and another group of activities related strictly to *Oedipus Rex* vocabulary.

Directions for these games, puzzles and worksheets are self-explanatory. The object here is to provide you with extra materials you may use in any way you choose.

Have students work together to make a time line chronology of the events in the story. Take a large piece of construction paper and on one wall (or however you can physically arrange it in your room) and make the events of the story along it. Students may want to add drawings or cut-out pictures to represent the events (as well as a written statement).

Have students design a book cover (front and back and inside flaps) for *Oedipus Rex*.

Have students create movie posters for *Oedipus Rex* with an all-star modern cast.

Analyze William Butler Yeats' poem "Oedipus at Colonus" for its use of poetic devices and connection to the story of Oedipus. Since the poem is in public domain, a copy is included in this LiPlan.

Have students explore satire (after all, this is a heavy tragedy and the unit could use some levity). Satirist Tom Lehrer wrote a song poking fun at the condition known as the "Oedipus Complex." Examine the lyrics for elements of satire. Students can examine social issues in both *Oedipus Rex* and in the world around them and create satirical scenes surrounding the issues. A copy of Tom Lehrer's lyrics is included in this LitPlan with permission from the author.

As long as students are examining satire, why not explore parody? Watch videos by Weird Al Yankovic and examine the social issues being made fun of ("Eat It," a parody of Michael Jackson's "Beat It," is a classic). Students can explore the issues in both *Oedipus Rex* and in the world around them. A list of parody titles created by some of my students is included below:

Kylie's "Drink, Drink" (from "Dance, Dance" by Fallout Boy) parodying teenage drinking

Tom's "Lie on the Couch All Day" (from "Bang on the Drum All Day" by Todd Rundgren) about couch potatoes

Joe's "Polluted Fields Forever" (from "Strawberry Fields Forever" by The Beatles) about the ecology

Kyle's "Forever High" (from "Forever Young" by Alpha Ville) parodying teenage drug use

Rachel's "Republican Man" (from "Piano Man" by Billy Joel) about the state of the union

Heather's "Through the Bars" (from "Through Glass" by Stone Sour) parodying alcoholism

Ashley's "Everyday Downloading It's a Shame" (from "Every Day is Exactly the Same" by Nine Inch Nails) about those who download music illegally from the Internet

Mariel's "All I Want For Christmas is a Pony" (from "All I Want For Christmas is You" by Mariah Carey) about spoiled kids who want to be handed everything at Christmas

Christian's "10 Wings" (from "One Week" by the Barenaked Ladies) parodying obesity

Alexa's "Coming From a Cell of a Cingular User" (from Lips of an Angel" by Hinder) lamenting Cingular's plan vs. Verizon's

Tim's "Smokin' in My Basement" (from "Proud Mary" by Credence Clearwater Revival) about the tobacco industry

Sarah's "Long Bright Night" (from the Christmas carole "Silent Night") about how students don't get enough sleep

Rachel's "Girls Just Want to Have Sun" (from "Girls Just Want to Have Fun" by Cyndi Lauper) about teenaged girls' obsession with tanning salons

Andrew's "Give Up, You're Done" (from "Father and Son" by Cat Stevens) parodying the perils of drug use

Eric's "'Cause I Had a Million Callers" (from "If I Had a Million Dollars' by the Barenaked Ladies) about obnoxious telemarketers

Brian's "Touch Me Baby" (from "Tell Me Baby" by the Red Hot Chili Peppers) parodying the charges against Michael Jackson

Karen's "Credit Card Bills" (from "Beverly Hills" by Weezer) about credit card woes

Chris' "The Tag Song" (from "The Sweater Song" by Undone) parodying how playground injuries have led to the banishment of playing tag

Gina's "Ain't No Other Bully" (from "Ain't No Other Man" by Christine Aguilera) about school bullies

Carly's "O-B-E-S-I-T-Y" (from "R-E-S-P-E-C-T" by Aretha Franklin) parodying America's obsession with food

Molly's "Unmerciful" (from "Unfaithful" by Rihanna) about deer hunting from a vegan perspective

Denise's "More Bills For Me" (from Disney's "Under the Sea" in *The Little Mermaid*) parodying overspending on credit

Kate's "If I Fell and Chose to Sue" (from "If I Fell in Love With You" by the Beatles) about the sue-happy frenzy taking place in America

Megan's "Get Me More" (from "Make Damn Sure" by Taking Back Sunday) about how kids want more and more stuff and then don't use it once they get it

Luke's "Eight Days I Eat" (from "Eight Days a Week" by the Beatles), another fast food parody

Maggie's "Yellow Nails and Yellow Teeth" (from "Yellow Submarine" by the Beatles) parodying the ill effects of smoking

"A Man Young And Old: XI. From Oedipus At Colonus" by William Butler Yeats

Endure what life God gives and ask no longer span;
Cease to remember the delights of youth, travel-wearied aged man;
Delight becomes death-longing if all longing else be vain.

Even from that delight memory treasures so,
Death, despair, division of families, all entanglements of mankind grow,
As that old wandering beggar and these God-hated children know.

In the long echoing street the laughing dancers throng,
The bride is carried to the bridegroom's chamber through torchlight and tumultuous song;
I celebrate the silent kiss that ends short life or long.

Never to have lived is best, ancient writers say;
Never to have drawn the breath of life, never to have looked into the eye of day;
The second best's a gay goodnight and quickly turn away.

"Oedipus Rex" by Tom Lehrer

From the Bible to the popular song,
There's one theme that we find right along.
Of all ideals they hail as good,
The most sublime is Motherhood.

There was a man, oh, who it seems,
Once carried this ideal to extremes.
He loved his mother and she loved him,
And yet his story is rather grim.

There once lived a man named Oedipus Rex.
You may have heard about his odd complex.
His name appears in Freud's index
'Cause he loved his mother.

His rivals used to say quite a bit,
That as a monarch he was most unfit.
But still in all they had to admit
That he loved his mother.

Yes he loved his mother like no other.
His daughter was his sister and his son was his brother.
One thing on which you can depend is,
He sure knew who a boy's best friend is!

When he found what he had done,
He tore his eyes out one by one.
A tragic end to a loyal son
Who loved his mother.

So be sweet and kind to Mother,
Now and then have a chat.
Buy her candy or some flowers or a brand new hat.
But maybe you had better let it go at that!

Or you may find yourself with a quite complex complex,
And you may end up like Oedipus.
I'd rather marry a duck-billed platypus,
Than end up like old Oedipus Rex.
The out-patients are out in force tonight, I see.

Oedipus Word List

No.	Word	Clue/Definition
1.	ANTIGONE	One of Oedipus's daughters
2.	ANTISTROPHE	Movement of the chorus from left to right across the stage
3.	APOLLO	He is most concerned about Laios's murder.
4.	ATHENA	The Chorus prays to ___. Artemis, & Apollo for help.
5.	BLINDS	Oedipus ___ himself with the brooches from Iocaste's dress.
6.	CATHARSIS	Purification of a character's emotions; an emotional release
7.	CHORAGOS	Leader of the chorus
8.	CORINTH	City in which Oedipus was raised
9.	CREON	He took over as the King of Thebes.
10.	DELPHI	Location of Apollo's temple
11.	DENOUEMENT	Resolution of the main conflict in a play
12.	EPISODE	Scene in a play
13.	EXILE	Oedipus follows his own edict and goes into self-___.
14.	EXODOS	Last song of the play, usually contains a moral lesson
15.	FURIES	They will follow the killer wherever he goes.
16.	HUBRIS	Arrogance demonstrated by a character as a result of pride or passion
17.	IOCASTE	Wife of Laios and Oedipus
18.	KITHAIRON	Infant Oedipus had been left in the shadow of Mt. ___.
19.	LAIOS	King of Thebes who was killed at a place where 3 roads meet
20.	LYING	The Chorus says that Teiresias is ___ in Ode I.
21.	MEROPE	Queen of Corinth feared by Oedipus
22.	ODES	Songs that comment on the action of the play or its characters
23.	OEDIPUS	Killed his father and married his mother
24.	PARODOS	Opening song as the chorus makes its entrance
25.	POLYBOS	King of Corinth who raised the abandoned infant Oedipus
26.	PROLOGUE	Introduces the main characters in the beginning of a play
27.	PROPHECY	A ___ had warned Oedipus of his fate.
28.	RELIEF	Feeling Oedipus has when he hears the King of Corinth is dead
29.	SATYR	Play that comically portrayed mythological stories or poked fun at politics
30.	SHEPHERD	A ___ spared infant Oedipus's life.
31.	SOPHOCLES	Author of Oedipus Rex
32.	SPHINX	Destroyed herself after Oedipus correctly answered her riddle
33.	STROPHE	Movement of the chorus from right to left across the stage
34.	SUICIDE	Iocaste commits this.
35.	TEIRESIAS	Blind prophet
36.	THEBES	City being destroyed by a plague because of an unsolved murder
37.	THESPIS	Father of Greek Theatre
38.	TRAGEDY	Serious play in which the main character suffers from a flaw
39.	TRAITOR	Oedipus accused Creon of being a ___ at the opening of Scene 2 Ode 2.

Oedipus Word Search

```
S P H I N X D E N O U E M E N T C P K K
P Q N B X W M D J K F D T A O P H R K N
S H C S P N X N G X U E H N E R O O G P
C A T H A R S I S F R L E T D O R P K D
X Y B D R F T H T B I P S I I L A H I D
S Q G R V V S E D Q E H P G P O G E T X
Y O B Z B N W M I Z S I I O U G O C H T
X D P G P N W V C R S R S N S U S Y A M
P Y W H B S B L B C E C V E L E E L I K
A N Q Y O B P M G V R S F T P Y X S R Z
R B F W B C O Q Z F Y S I R T O O P O B
O H L C N X L Y I N G T R A G E D Y N D
D D S I R D Y E X L F N D I S H O E Q X
O Y G R N E B W S S M L P T D S S S S R
S A T Y R D O A T H E N A O E X I L E R
H U J Q R L S N R E R L X R S Q O A P T
U C I H E M S W O P O G B P Q C C I I Y
B L B C L B D C P H P S F C N Y A O S L
R C O R I N T H H E E T H E B E S S O L
I M J C E D Y C E R X Q N D V Q T P D H
S F Q T F B E T H D A P O L L O E B E R
```

ANTIGONE	DELPHI	KITHAIRON	PROLOGUE	SUICIDE
APOLLO	DENOUEMENT	LAIOS	PROPHECY	TEIRESIAS
ATHENA	EPISODE	LYING	RELIEF	THEBES
BLINDS	EXILE	MEROPE	SATYR	THESPIS
CATHARSIS	EXODOS	ODES	SHEPHERD	TRAGEDY
CHORAGOS	FURIES	OEDIPUS	SOPHOCLES	TRAITOR
CORINTH	HUBRIS	PARODOS	SPHINX	
CREON	IOCASTE	POLYBOS	STROPHE	

Oedipus Word Search Answer Key

ANTIGONE	DELPHI	KITHAIRON	PROLOGUE	SUICIDE
APOLLO	DENOUEMENT	LAIOS	PROPHECY	TEIRESIAS
ATHENA	EPISODE	LYING	RELIEF	THEBES
BLINDS	EXILE	MEROPE	SATYR	THESPIS
CATHARSIS	EXODOS	ODES	SHEPHERD	TRAGEDY
CHORAGOS	FURIES	OEDIPUS	SOPHOCLES	TRAITOR
CORINTH	HUBRIS	PARODOS	SPHINX	
CREON	IOCASTE	POLYBOS	STROPHE	

Oedipus Crossword

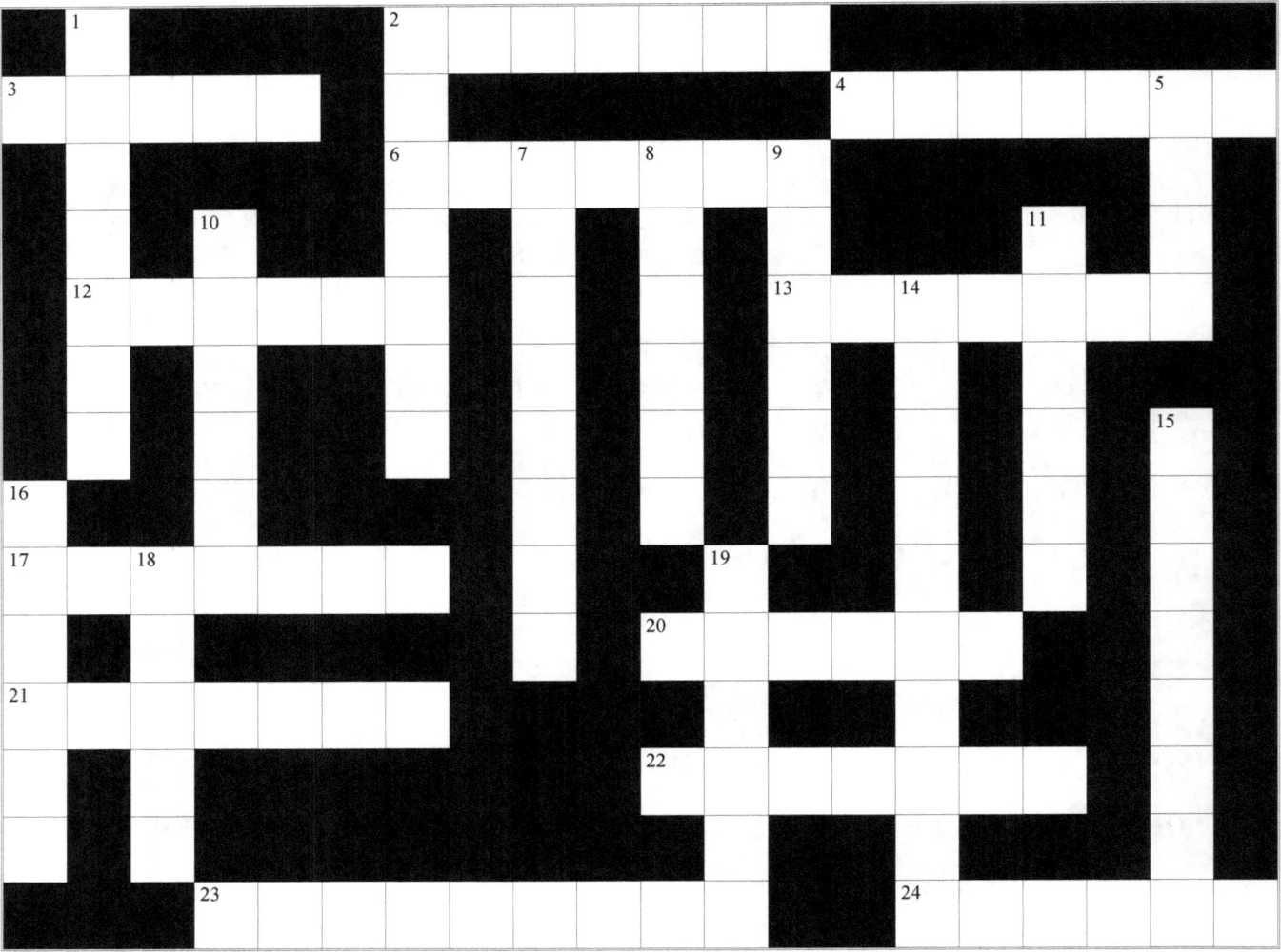

Across
2. Movement of the chorus from right to left across the stage
3. Play that comically portrayed mythological stories or poked fun at politics
4. Oedipus accused Creon of being a ___ at the opening of Scene 2 Ode 2.
6. Wife of Laios and Oedipus
12. Location of Apollo's temple
13. Killed his father and married his mother
17. Father of Greek Theatre
20. They will follow the killer wherever he goes.
21. Scene in a play
22. Serious play in which the main character suffers from a flaw
23. Purification of a character's emotions; an emotional release
24. City being destroyed by a plague because of an unsolved murder

Down
1. Opening song as the chorus makes its entrance
2. Iocaste commits this.
5. Songs that comment on the action of the play or its characters
7. Leader of the chorus
8. Destroyed herself after Oedipus correctly answered her riddle
9. Last song of the play, usually contains a moral lesson
10. Oedipus ___ himself with the brooches from Iocaste's dress.
11. He is most concerned about Laios's murder.
14. Resolution of the main conflict in a play
15. One of Oedipus's daughters
16. The Chorus prays to ___. Artemis, & Apollo for help.
18. Oedipus follows his own edict and goes into self-___.
19. Arrogance demonstrated by a character as a result of pride or passion

Oedipus Crossword Answer Key

	1 P		2 S	T	R	O	P	H	E			4 T	R	5 A	I	T	O	R
3 S	A	T	Y	R														
	R			6 I	7 O	C	A	8 S	T	9 E								D
	O		10 B		C			H		P				11 A				E
	12 D	E	L	P	H	I		O		13 O	E	14 D	I	P	U	S		
	O		I			D		R		D		E		O				
	S		N			E		A		I		N		L				15 A
16 A			D					G		N		O		L				N
17 T	H	18 E	S	P	I	S		O		19 H		U		O				T
H		X						S		20 F	U	R	I	E	S			I
21 E	P	I	S	O	D	E				B		M						G
N		L								22 T	R	A	G	E	D	Y		O
A		E								I		N						N
		23 C	A	T	H	A	R	S	I	S		24 T	H	E	B	E	S	

Across
2. Movement of the chorus from right to left across the stage
3. Play that comically portrayed mythological stories or poked fun at politics
4. Oedipus accused Creon of being a ___ at the opening of Scene 2 Ode 2.
6. Wife of Laios and Oedipus
12. Location of Apollo's temple
13. Killed his father and married his mother
17. Father of Greek Theatre
20. They will follow the killer wherever he goes.
21. Scene in a play
22. Serious play in which the main character suffers from a flaw
23. Purification of a character's emotions; an emotional release
24. City being destroyed by a plague because of an unsolved murder

Down
1. Opening song as the chorus makes its entrance
2. Iocaste commits this.
5. Songs that comment on the action of the play or its characters
7. Leader of the chorus
8. Destroyed herself after Oedipus correctly answered her riddle
9. Last song of the play, usually contains a moral lesson
10. Oedipus ___ himself with the brooches from Iocaste's dress.
11. He is most concerned about Laios's murder.
14. Resolution of the main conflict in a play
15. One of Oedipus's daughters
16. The Chorus prays to ___, Artemis, & Apollo for help.
18. Oedipus follows his own edict and goes into self-___.
19. Arrogance demonstrated by a character as a result of pride or passion

Oedipus Matching 1

___ 1. HUBRIS A. City in which Oedipus was raised
___ 2. LAIOS B. Leader of the chorus
___ 3. ODES C. Oedipus follows his own edict and goes into self-___.
___ 4. EPISODE D. Songs that comment on the action of the play or its characters
___ 5. PROLOGUE E. Serious play in which the main character suffers from a flaw
___ 6. OEDIPUS F. They will follow the killer wherever he goes.
___ 7. STROPHE G. A ___ spared infant Oedipus's life.
___ 8. IOCASTE H. Introduces the main characters in the beginning of a play
___ 9. MEROPE I. Movement of the chorus from left to right across the stage
___10. THESPIS J. King of Corinth who raised the abandoned infant Oedipus
___11. KITHAIRON K. Resolution of the main conflict in a play
___12. CREON L. Arrogance demonstrated by a character as a result of pride or passion
___13. EXILE M. Movement of the chorus from right to left across the stage
___14. RELIEF N. Scene in a play
___15. DENOUEMENT O. Destroyed herself after Oedipus correctly answered her riddle
___16. ANTIGONE P. Father of Greek Theatre
___17. TRAGEDY Q. King of Thebes who was killed at a place where 3 roads meet
___18. CORINTH R. Feeling Oedipus has when he hears the King of Corinth is dead
___19. SHEPHERD S. Wife of Laios and Oedipus
___20. ANTISTROPHE T. Queen of Corinth feared by Oedipus
___21. CHORAGOS U. Purification of a character's emotions; an emotional release
___22. FURIES V. Killed his father and married his mother
___23. POLYBOS W. Infant Oedipus had been left in the shadow of Mt. ___.
___24. SPHINX X. He took over as the King of Thebes.
___25. CATHARSIS Y. One of Oedipus's daughters

Oedipus Matching 1 Answer Key

L - 1.	HUBRIS	A. City in which Oedipus was raised
Q - 2.	LAIOS	B. Leader of the chorus
D - 3.	ODES	C. Oedipus follows his own edict and goes into self-___.
N - 4.	EPISODE	D. Songs that comment on the action of the play or its characters
H - 5.	PROLOGUE	E. Serious play in which the main character suffers from a flaw
V - 6.	OEDIPUS	F. They will follow the killer wherever he goes.
M - 7.	STROPHE	G. A ___ spared infant Oedipus's life.
S - 8.	IOCASTE	H. Introduces the main characters in the beginning of a play
T - 9.	MEROPE	I. Movement of the chorus from left to right across the stage
P - 10.	THESPIS	J. King of Corinth who raised the abandoned infant Oedipus
W - 11.	KITHAIRON	K. Resolution of the main conflict in a play
X - 12.	CREON	L. Arrogance demonstrated by a character as a result of pride or passion
C - 13.	EXILE	M. Movement of the chorus from right to left across the stage
R - 14.	RELIEF	N. Scene in a play
K - 15.	DENOUEMENT	O. Destroyed herself after Oedipus correctly answered her riddle
Y - 16.	ANTIGONE	P. Father of Greek Theatre
E - 17.	TRAGEDY	Q. King of Thebes who was killed at a place where 3 roads meet
A - 18.	CORINTH	R. Feeling Oedipus has when he hears the King of Corinth is dead
G - 19.	SHEPHERD	S. Wife of Laios and Oedipus
I - 20.	ANTISTROPHE	T. Queen of Corinth feared by Oedipus
B - 21.	CHORAGOS	U. Purification of a character's emotions; an emotional release
F - 22.	FURIES	V. Killed his father and married his mother
J - 23.	POLYBOS	W. Infant Oedipus had been left in the shadow of Mt. ___.
O - 24.	SPHINX	X. He took over as the King of Thebes.
U - 25.	CATHARSIS	Y. One of Oedipus's daughters

Oedipus Matching 2

___ 1. DELPHI A. Destroyed herself after Oedipus correctly answered her riddle
___ 2. KITHAIRON B. Feeling Oedipus has when he hears the King of Corinth is dead
___ 3. SOPHOCLES C. Wife of Laios and Oedipus
___ 4. BLINDS D. Oedipus follows his own edict and goes into self-___.
___ 5. TRAITOR E. King of Corinth who raised the abandoned infant Oedipus
___ 6. TEIRESIAS F. A ___ had warned Oedipus of his fate.
___ 7. SHEPHERD G. They will follow the killer wherever he goes.
___ 8. SPHINX H. Queen of Corinth feared by Oedipus
___ 9. FURIES I. The Chorus says that Teiresias is ___ in Ode I.
___10. PROPHECY J. Oedipus accused Creon of being a ___ at the opening of Scene 2 Ode 2.
___11. RELIEF K. City being destroyed by a plague because of an unsolved murder
___12. CORINTH L. Iocaste commits this.
___13. OEDIPUS M. Location of Apollo's temple
___14. IOCASTE N. King of Thebes who was killed at a place where 3 roads meet
___15. CREON O. One of Oedipus's daughters
___16. THEBES P. He is most concerned about Laios's murder.
___17. SUICIDE Q. Killed his father and married his mother
___18. ATHENA R. Oedipus ___ himself with the brooches from Iocaste's dress.
___19. MEROPE S. He took over as the King of Thebes.
___20. EXILE T. Infant Oedipus had been left in the shadow of Mt. ___.
___21. POLYBOS U. City in which Oedipus was raised
___22. APOLLO V. The Chorus prays to ___. Artemis, & Apollo for help.
___23. LYING W. A ___ spared infant Oedipus's life.
___24. LAIOS X. Blind prophet
___25. ANTIGONE Y. Author of Oedipus Rex

Oedipus Matching 2 Answer Key

M - 1.	DELPHI	A. Destroyed herself after Oedipus correctly answered her riddle
T - 2.	KITHAIRON	B. Feeling Oedipus has when he hears the King of Corinth is dead
Y - 3.	SOPHOCLES	C. Wife of Laios and Oedipus
R - 4.	BLINDS	D. Oedipus follows his own edict and goes into self-___.
J - 5.	TRAITOR	E. King of Corinth who raised the abandoned infant Oedipus
X - 6.	TEIRESIAS	F. A ___ had warned Oedipus of his fate.
W - 7.	SHEPHERD	G. They will follow the killer wherever he goes.
A - 8.	SPHINX	H. Queen of Corinth feared by Oedipus
G - 9.	FURIES	I. The Chorus says that Teiresias is ___ in Ode I.
F - 10.	PROPHECY	J. Oedipus accused Creon of being a ___ at the opening of Scene 2 Ode 2.
B - 11.	RELIEF	K. City being destroyed by a plague because of an unsolved murder
U - 12.	CORINTH	L. Iocaste commits this.
Q - 13.	OEDIPUS	M. Location of Apollo's temple
C - 14.	IOCASTE	N. King of Thebes who was killed at a place where 3 roads meet
S - 15.	CREON	O. One of Oedipus's daughters
K - 16.	THEBES	P. He is most concerned about Laios's murder.
L - 17.	SUICIDE	Q. Killed his father and married his mother
V - 18.	ATHENA	R. Oedipus ___ himself with the brooches from Iocaste's dress.
H - 19.	MEROPE	S. He took over as the King of Thebes.
D - 20.	EXILE	T. Infant Oedipus had been left in the shadow of Mt. ___.
E - 21.	POLYBOS	U. City in which Oedipus was raised
P - 22.	APOLLO	V. The Chorus prays to ___. Artemis, & Apollo for help.
I - 23.	LYING	W. A ___ spared infant Oedipus's life.
N - 24.	LAIOS	X. Blind prophet
O - 25.	ANTIGONE	Y. Author of Oedipus Rex

Oedipus Juggle Letters

1. XELIE = 1. _____
   Oedipus follows his own edict and goes into self-___.

2. PDELHI = 2. _____
   Location of Apollo's temple

3. HBESET = 3. _____
   City being destroyed by a plague because of an unsolved murder

4. ATAENH = 4. _____
   The Chorus prays to ___. Artemis, & Apollo for help.

5. OILSA = 5. _____
   King of Thebes who was killed at a place where 3 roads meet

6. NSBIDL = 6. _____
   Oedipus ___ himself with the brooches from Iocaste's dress.

7. IOHKTANRI = 7. _____
   Infant Oedipus had been left in the shadow of Mt. ___.

8. ICTHRON = 8. _____
   City in which Oedipus was raised

9. POCHRYPE = 9. _____
   A ___ had warned Oedipus of his fate.

10. BLYPOSO =10. _____
    King of Corinth who raised the abandoned infant Oedipus

11. EHDRSEHP =11. _____
    A ___ spared infant Oedipus's life.

12. ROEPME =12. _____
    Queen of Corinth feared by Oedipus

13. NLGYI =13. _____
    The Chorus says that Teiresias is ___ in Ode I.

14. OPLEOHSCS =14. _____
    Author of Oedipus Rex

15. ONRCE =15. _____
    He took over as the King of Thebes.

16. LLOOAP =16. _____
He is most concerned about Laios's murder.

17. GAIOTENN =17. _____
One of Oedipus's daughters

18. ATCIEOS =18. _____
Wife of Laios and Oedipus

19. DUIOEPS =19. _____
Killed his father and married his mother

20. USDIEIC =20. _____
Iocaste commits this.

21. NIXPSH =21. _____
Destroyed herself after Oedipus correctly answered her riddle

22. EEFLRI =22. _____
Feeling Oedipus has when he hears the King of Corinth is dead

23. RIOTTRA =23. _____
Oedipus accused Creon of being a ___ at the opening of Scene 2 Ode 2.

Oedipus Juggle Letters Answer Key

1. XELIE = 1. EXILE
   Oedipus follows his own edict and goes into self-___.

2. PDELHI = 2. DELPHI
   Location of Apollo's temple

3. HBESET = 3. THEBES
   City being destroyed by a plague because of an unsolved murder

4. ATAENH = 4. ATHENA
   The Chorus prays to ___. Artemis, & Apollo for help.

5. OILSA = 5. LAIOS
   King of Thebes who was killed at a place where 3 roads meet

6. NSBIDL = 6. BLINDS
   Oedipus ___ himself with the brooches from Iocaste's dress.

7. IOHKTANRI = 7. KITHAIRON
   Infant Oedipus had been left in the shadow of Mt. ___.

8. ICTHRON = 8. CORINTH
   City in which Oedipus was raised

9. POCHRYPE = 9. PROPHECY
   A ___ had warned Oedipus of his fate.

10. BLYPOSO = 10. POLYBOS
    King of Corinth who raised the abandoned infant Oedipus

11. EHDRSEHP = 11. SHEPHERD
    A ___ spared infant Oedipus's life.

12. ROEPME = 12. MEROPE
    Queen of Corinth feared by Oedipus

13. NLGYI = 13. LYING
    The Chorus says that Teiresias is ___ in Ode I.

14. OPLEOHSCS = 14. SOPHOCLES
    Author of Oedipus Rex

15. ONRCE = 15. CREON
    He took over as the King of Thebes.

16. LLOOAP =16. APOLLO

He is most concerned about Laios's murder.

17. GAIOTENN =17. ANTIGONE

One of Oedipus's daughters

18. ATCIEOS =18. IOCASTE

Wife of Laios and Oedipus

19. DUIOEPS =19. OEDIPUS

Killed his father and married his mother

20. USDIEIC =20. SUICIDE

Iocaste commits this.

21. NIXPSH =21. SPHINX

Destroyed herself after Oedipus correctly answered her riddle

22. EEFLRI =22. RELIEF

Feeling Oedipus has when he hears the King of Corinth is dead

23. RIOTTRA =23. TRAITOR

Oedipus accused Creon of being a ___ at the opening of Scene 2 Ode 2.

VOCABULARY RESOURCE MATERIALS

Oedipus Vocabulary Word List

No.	Word	Clue/Definition
1.	ABOMINATION	Anything greatly disliked or abhorred
2.	AUGURY	An event indicating important things to come: fortune telling
3.	BANE	A person or thing that ruins or spoils
4.	BASENESS	Characteristic of or befitting an inferior person or thing
5.	BATTENS	To thrive and prosper, especially at another's expense
6.	BEGETTING	Fathering; siring
7.	BESIEGER	An enemy who lays siege to your positions
8.	BRAZEN	Boldly shameless or impudent
9.	BROOCHES	Relatively large decorative pins or clasps
10.	COMPUNCTION	Any uneasiness or hesitation about the rightness of an action
11.	CONTAGION	The means by which a contagious disease is transmitted
12.	DECREPIT	Weakened by old age; feeble
13.	DEFILEMENT	To make foul, dirty, or unclean; pollute
14.	DIN	A loud, disturbing noise
15.	EASE	Freedom from difficulty or great effort
16.	EDICT	Any authoritative proclamation or command
17.	ENQUIRY	A seeking or request for truth, information, or knowledge
18.	EXECRABLE	Utterly detestable; abominable; very bad
19.	EXPELLED	Forced or drove out
20.	FACTION	A group or clique within a larger group, party, or government
21.	FRAILTY	Moral weakness; liability to yield to temptation
22.	GROUNDLESS	Without rational basis
23.	HARROWED	To break up soil with a toll consisting of a heavy frame with sharp teeth
24.	HEARTH	The floor of a fireplace, usually of stone or brick
25.	HELMSMAN	A person who steers a ship
26.	INSOLENCE	Rude or impertinent behavior or speech
27.	ISTHMUS	A narrow strip of land, bordered on both sides by water, connecting two larger bodies of land
28.	LIBERATOR	Someone who releases people from captivity or bondage
29.	LUSTRATION	The act of purifying by means of ceremony
30.	MALEDICTION	The utterance of a curse
31.	MAUNDERING	Moving or acting in an aimless or vague manner
32.	MUMMERY	Any performance or ceremony regarded as absurd or false
33.	NYMPHS	Female spirits who lived in forests, bodies of water, and other places outdoors
34.	OUTCAST	One who is rejected or discarded
35.	OVERWROUGHT	Extremely or excessively excited or agitated
36.	PARRICIDE	A person who kills his own parent
37.	PARRY	To turn aside; evade or dodge
38.	PASTURAGE	The activity or business of pasturing livestock
39.	PERQUISITES	Those things claimed as exclusive rights
40.	PESTILENCE	Something that is considered harmful, destructive, or evil
41.	PRESUME	To take for granted, assume, or suppose
42.	PRIMAL	Being first in time; original
43.	PRUDENT	Wise or judicious in practical affairs
44.	RANKLED	Caused keen irritation or bitter resentment
45.	REASSURED	Restored confidence to
46.	RENOWN	Widespread and high repute; fame
47.	REGICIDE	The killing of a king
48.	SCANT	To treat slightly or inadequately
49.	SEPULCHRE	A tomb, grave, or burial place

Oedipus Vocabulary Word List Continued

50. SHROUD — A cloth or sheet in which a corpse is wrapped for burial
51. SIRING — A father's children
52. SOLEMN — Causing serious thoughts or a grave mood
53. SOOTHSAYER — Person who professes to foretell events, fortune-teller
54. SPLENDOR — Brilliant or gorgeous appearance
55. SUPPLIANT — One who asks humbly and earnestly
56. SUPPLICATION — To ask for humbly or earnestly, as by praying
57. VENERATE — To regard or treat with reverence or respect
58. VIGIL — A period of watchful attention maintained at night
59. VOID — An empty space; emptiness
60. WRETCHED — Very unfortunate in condition or circumstances

Oedipus Vocabulary Word Search

```
P  M  E  X  P  E  L  L  E  D  R  B  A  S  E  N  E  S  S  W
A  A  S  O  O  T  H  S  A  Y  E  R  R  K  N  Y  M  P  H  S
R  U  Y  V  F  F  J  R  P  X  G  J  G  L  Z  Q  H  L  G  R
R  N  X  W  A  W  S  E  X  H  I  D  Y  A  S  O  L  E  M  N
Y  D  F  X  C  T  J  N  X  G  C  B  X  W  U  H  L  N  Z  R
B  E  B  K  T  R  R  O  W  P  I  W  E  X  L  G  R  D  K  Z
L  R  M  M  I  H  A  W  V  B  D  X  B  S  Q  Q  U  O  X  R
D  I  N  S  O  L  E  N  C  E  E  N  Q  U  I  R  Y  R  U  V
E  N  B  B  N  U  P  S  K  D  G  G  S  I  B  E  B  K  Y  D
C  G  Z  E  A  V  T  R  C  L  N  M  E  S  Y  R  G  A  Y  R
R  H  E  A  R  T  H  C  I  A  E  V  P  T  S  K  A  E  N  S
E  R  G  D  S  A  T  D  A  M  N  D  U  H  T  G  D  Z  R  E
P  V  R  C  I  U  T  E  Z  S  A  T  L  M  G  I  I  V  E  P
I  E  O  P  O  C  P  O  N  P  T  L  C  U  L  S  N  I  D  N
T  N  U  I  E  N  T  P  R  S  W  N  H  S  U  U  H  G  E  G
B  E  N  W  D  S  T  P  L  F  E  P  R  M  S  P  A  I  F  C
R  R  D  F  R  Y  T  A  R  I  C  A  E  N  T  P  R  L  I  H
O  A  L  L  R  E  S  I  G  U  C  Y  S  P  R  L  R  S  L  D
O  T  E  R  F  A  T  V  L  I  D  A  Z  E  A  I  O  I  E  Y
C  E  S  B  Z  V  I  C  P  E  O  E  T  D  T  A  W  R  M  H
H  F  S  F  G  T  D  L  H  Q  N  N  N  I  I  N  E  I  E  V
E  P  R  E  S  U  M  E  T  E  Z  C  Q  T  O  T  D  N  N  G
S  M  U  M  M  E  R  Y  J  Y  D  Y  E  G  N  N  K  G  T  Q
```

AUGURY	DEFILEMENT	HEARTH	PESTILENCE	SIRING
BANE	DIN	INSOLENCE	PRESUME	SOLEMN
BASENESS	EASE	ISTHMUS	PRIMAL	SOOTHSAYER
BATTENS	EDICT	LIBERATOR	PRUDENT	SPLENDOR
BEGETTING	ENQUIRY	LUSTRATION	RANKLED	SUPPLIANT
BESIEGER	EXPELLED	MAUNDERING	REGICIDE	SUPPLICATION
BRAZEN	FACTION	MUMMERY	RENOWN	VENERATE
BROOCHES	FRAILTY	NYMPHS	SCANT	VIGIL
CONTAGION	GROUNDLESS	OUTCAST	SEPULCHRE	VOID
DECREPIT	HARROWED	PARRY	SHROUD	WRETCHED

Oedipus Vocabulary Word Search Answer Key

AUGURY	DEFILEMENT	HEARTH	PESTILENCE	SIRING
BANE	DIN	INSOLENCE	PRESUME	SOLEMN
BASENESS	EASE	ISTHMUS	PRIMAL	SOOTHSAYER
BATTENS	EDICT	LIBERATOR	PRUDENT	SPLENDOR
BEGETTING	ENQUIRY	LUSTRATION	RANKLED	SUPPLIANT
BESIEGER	EXPELLED	MAUNDERING	REGICIDE	SUPPLICATION
BRAZEN	FACTION	MUMMERY	RENOWN	VENERATE
BROOCHES	FRAILTY	NYMPHS	SCANT	VIGIL
CONTAGION	GROUNDLESS	OUTCAST	SEPULCHRE	VOID
DECREPIT	HARROWED	PARRY	SHROUD	WRETCHED

Oedipus Vocabulary Crossword

Across
6. Being first in time; original
7. Those things claimed as exclusive rights
8. Freedom from difficulty or great effort
9. To thrive and prosper, especially at another's expense
11. Any authoritative proclamation or command
13. Moral weakness; liability to yield to temptation
15. To turn aside; evade or dodge
16. Female spirits who lived in forests, bodies of water, and other places outdoors
18. To treat slightly or inadequately
19. An event indicating important things to come: fortune telling
20. Widespread and high repute; fame
21. Utterly detestable; abominable; very bad
22. A seeking or request for truth, information, or knowledge

Down
1. Without rational basis
2. A person or thing that ruins or spoils
3. A loud, disturbing noise
4. A period of watchful attention maintained at night
5. The floor of a fireplace, usually of stone or brick
7. Something that is considered harmful, destructive, or evil
9. Boldly shameless or impudent
10. Person who professes to foretell events, fortune-teller
12. The means by which a contagious disease is transmitted
13. A group or clique within a larger group, party, or government
14. The activity or business of pasturing livestock
17. Any performance or ceremony regarded as absurd or false

Oedipus Vocabulary Crossword Answer Key

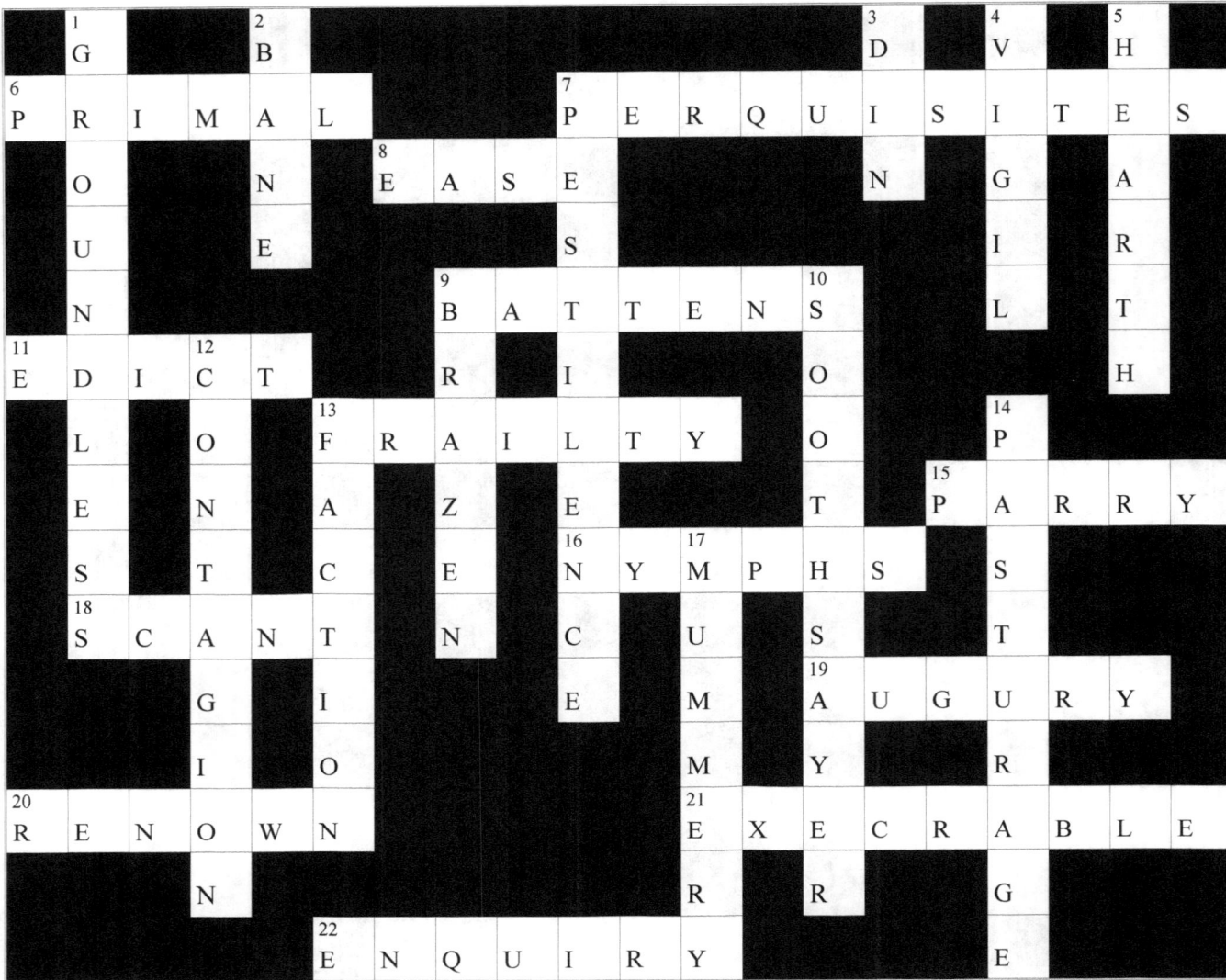

Across
- 6. Being first in time; original
- 7. Those things claimed as exclusive rights
- 8. Freedom from difficulty or great effort
- 9. To thrive and prosper, especially at another's expense
- 11. Any authoritative proclamation or command
- 13. Moral weakness; liability to yield to temptation
- 15. To turn aside; evade or dodge
- 16. Female spirits who lived in forests, bodies of water, and other places outdoors
- 18. To treat slightly or inadequately
- 19. An event indicating important things to come: fortune telling
- 20. Widespread and high repute; fame
- 21. Utterly detestable; abominable; very bad
- 22. A seeking or request for truth, information, or knowledge

Down
- 1. Without rational basis
- 2. A person or thing that ruins or spoils
- 3. A loud, disturbing noise
- 4. A period of watchful attention maintained at night
- 5. The floor of a fireplace, usually of stone or brick
- 7. Something that is considered harmful, destructive, or evil
- 9. Boldly shameless or impudent
- 10. Person who professes to foretell events, fortune-teller
- 12. The means by which a contagious disease is transmitted
- 13. A group or clique within a larger group, party, or government
- 14. The activity or business of pasturing livestock
- 17. Any performance or ceremony regarded as absurd or false

Oedipus Vocabulary Matching 1

___ 1. SUPPLIANT   A. To turn aside; evade or dodge
___ 2. MALEDICTION   B. An enemy who lays siege to your positions
___ 3. REASSURED   C. A person who steers a ship
___ 4. EXPELLED   D. Being first in time; original
___ 5. INSOLENCE   E. A father's children
___ 6. EXECRABLE   F. Relatively large decorative pins or clasps
___ 7. BEGETTING   G. Restored confidence to
___ 8. OVERWROUGHT   H. Those things claimed as exclusive rights
___ 9. WRETCHED   I. Fathering; siring
___10. RENOWN   J. Utterly detestable; abominable; very bad
___11. VOID   K. The utterance of a curse
___12. LIBERATOR   L. Very unfortunate in condition or circumstances
___13. PRESUME   M. Someone who releases people from captivity or bondage
___14. LUSTRATION   N. A group or clique within a larger group, party, or government
___15. VENERATE   O. Forced or drove out
___16. SCANT   P. To regard or treat with reverence or respect
___17. SIRING   Q. Widespread and high repute; fame
___18. AUGURY   R. Rude or impertinent behavior or speech
___19. HELMSMAN   S. To treat slightly or inadequately
___20. BESIEGER   T. One who asks humbly and earnestly
___21. PARRY   U. An event indicating important things to come: fortune telling
___22. FACTION   V. To take for granted, assume, or suppose
___23. BROOCHES   W. The act of purifying by means of ceremony
___24. PERQUISITES   X. Extremely or excessively excited or agitated
___25. PRIMAL   Y. An empty space; emptiness

Oedipus Vocabulary Matching 1 Answer Key

T - 1.	SUPPLIANT	A. To turn aside; evade or dodge
K - 2.	MALEDICTION	B. An enemy who lays siege to your positions
G - 3.	REASSURED	C. A person who steers a ship
O - 4.	EXPELLED	D. Being first in time; original
R - 5.	INSOLENCE	E. A father's children
J - 6.	EXECRABLE	F. Relatively large decorative pins or clasps
I - 7.	BEGETTING	G. Restored confidence to
X - 8.	OVERWROUGHT	H. Those things claimed as exclusive rights
L - 9.	WRETCHED	I. Fathering; siring
Q -10.	RENOWN	J. Utterly detestable; abominable; very bad
Y -11.	VOID	K. The utterance of a curse
M -12.	LIBERATOR	L. Very unfortunate in condition or circumstances
V -13.	PRESUME	M. Someone who releases people from captivity or bondage
W -14.	LUSTRATION	N. A group or clique within a larger group, party, or government
P -15.	VENERATE	O. Forced or drove out
S -16.	SCANT	P. To regard or treat with reverence or respect
E -17.	SIRING	Q. Widespread and high repute; fame
U -18.	AUGURY	R. Rude or impertinent behavior or speech
C -19.	HELMSMAN	S. To treat slightly or inadequately
B -20.	BESIEGER	T. One who asks humbly and earnestly
A -21.	PARRY	U. An event indicating important things to come: fortune telling
N -22.	FACTION	V. To take for granted, assume, or suppose
F -23.	BROOCHES	W. The act of purifying by means of ceremony
H -24.	PERQUISITES	X. Extremely or excessively excited or agitated
D -25.	PRIMAL	Y. An empty space; emptiness

Oedipus Vocabulary Matching 2

___ 1. LUSTRATION	A. Very unfortunate in condition or circumstances
___ 2. PERQUISITES	B. Weakened by old age; feeble
___ 3. PRESUME	C. An empty space; emptiness
___ 4. VOID	D. Those things claimed as exclusive rights
___ 5. DECREPIT	E. A person or thing that ruins or spoils
___ 6. REASSURED	F. One who is rejected or discarded
___ 7. FRAILTY	G. A narrow strip of land, bordered on both sides by water, connecting two larger bodies of land
___ 8. EXPELLED	H. A period of watchful attention maintained at night
___ 9. SHROUD	I. Someone who releases people from captivity or bondage
___ 10. PARRICIDE	J. Moral weakness; liability to yield to temptation
___ 11. PRIMAL	K. To ask for humbly or earnestly, as by praying
___ 12. EXECRABLE	L. A person who kills his own parent
___ 13. NYMPHS	M. Utterly detestable; abominable; very bad
___ 14. BANE	N. A cloth or sheet in which a corpse is wrapped for burial
___ 15. WRETCHED	O. Boldly shameless or impudent
___ 16. SUPPLICATION	P. Caused keen irritation or bitter resentment
___ 17. BRAZEN	Q. To take for granted, assume, or suppose
___ 18. BESIEGER	R. Forced or drove out
___ 19. LIBERATOR	S. The utterance of a curse
___ 20. MALEDICTION	T. To turn aside; evade or dodge
___ 21. ISTHMUS	U. An enemy who lays siege to your positions
___ 22. VIGIL	V. Restored confidence to
___ 23. OUTCAST	W. The act of purifying by means of ceremony
___ 24. RANKLED	X. Being first in time; original
___ 25. PARRY	Y. Female spirits who lived in forests, bodies of water, and other places outdoors

Oedipus Vocabulary Matching 2 Answer Key

W	1. LUSTRATION	A.	Very unfortunate in condition or circumstances
D	2. PERQUISITES	B.	Weakened by old age; feeble
Q	3. PRESUME	C.	An empty space; emptiness
C	4. VOID	D.	Those things claimed as exclusive rights
B	5. DECREPIT	E.	A person or thing that ruins or spoils
V	6. REASSURED	F.	One who is rejected or discarded
J	7. FRAILTY	G.	A narrow strip of land, bordered on both sides by water, connecting two larger bodies of land
R	8. EXPELLED	H.	A period of watchful attention maintained at night
N	9. SHROUD	I.	Someone who releases people from captivity or bondage
L	10. PARRICIDE	J.	Moral weakness; liability to yield to temptation
X	11. PRIMAL	K.	To ask for humbly or earnestly, as by praying
M	12. EXECRABLE	L.	A person who kills his own parent
Y	13. NYMPHS	M.	Utterly detestable; abominable; very bad
E	14. BANE	N.	A cloth or sheet in which a corpse is wrapped for burial
A	15. WRETCHED	O.	Boldly shameless or impudent
K	16. SUPPLICATION	P.	Caused keen irritation or bitter resentment
O	17. BRAZEN	Q.	To take for granted, assume, or suppose
U	18. BESIEGER	R.	Forced or drove out
I	19. LIBERATOR	S.	The utterance of a curse
S	20. MALEDICTION	T.	To turn aside; evade or dodge
G	21. ISTHMUS	U.	An enemy who lays siege to your positions
H	22. VIGIL	V.	Restored confidence to
F	23. OUTCAST	W.	The act of purifying by means of ceremony
P	24. RANKLED	X.	Being first in time; original
T	25. PARRY	Y.	Female spirits who lived in forests, bodies of water, and other places outdoors

Oedipus Vocabulary Juggle Letters 1

1. TLESENPEIC = 1. _____
   Something that is considered harmful, destructive, or evil

2. SIOTLTUNAR = 2. _____
   The act of purifying by means of ceremony

3. NITFAOC = 3. _____
   A group or clique within a larger group, party, or government

4. EBEIERSG = 4. _____
   An enemy who lays siege to your positions

5. HSITSMU = 5. _____
   A narrow strip of land, bordered on both sides by water, connecting two larger bodies of land

6. PCDETRIE = 6. _____
   Weakened by old age; feeble

7. DUEARESRS = 7. _____
   Restored confidence to

8. BNEGIGETT = 8. _____
   Fathering; siring

9. PANLSPUIT = 9. _____
   One who asks humbly and earnestly

10. ARMPIL = 10. _____
    Being first in time; original

11. EAELRECBX = 11. _____
    Utterly detestable; abominable; very bad

12. AEES = 12. _____
    Freedom from difficulty or great effort

13. AWOEDRHR = 13. _____
    To break up soil with a toll consisting of a heavy frame with sharp teeth

14. ASTHEOSYOR = 14. _____
    Person who professes to foretell events, fortune-teller

Oedipus Vocabulary Juggle Letters 1 Answer Key

1. TLESENPEIC = 1. PESTILENCE
Something that is considered harmful, destructive, or evil

2. SIOTLTUNAR = 2. LUSTRATION
The act of purifying by means of ceremony

3. NITFAOC = 3. FACTION
A group or clique within a larger group, party, or government

4. EBEIERSG = 4. BESIEGER
An enemy who lays siege to your positions

5. HSITSMU = 5. ISTHMUS
A narrow strip of land, bordered on both sides by water, connecting two larger bodies of land

6. PCDETRIE = 6. DECREPIT
Weakened by old age; feeble

7. DUEARESRS = 7. REASSURED
Restored confidence to

8. BNEGIGETT = 8. BEGETTING
Fathering; siring

9. PANLSPUIT = 9. SUPPLIANT
One who asks humbly and earnestly

10. ARMPIL = 10. PRIMAL
Being first in time; original

11. EAELRECBX = 11. EXECRABLE
Utterly detestable; abominable; very bad

12. AEES = 12. EASE
Freedom from difficulty or great effort

13. AWOEDRHR = 13. HARROWED
To break up soil with a toll consisting of a heavy frame with sharp teeth

14. ASTHEOSYOR = 14. SOOTHSAYER
Person who professes to foretell events, fortune-teller

Oedipus Vocabulary Juggle Letters 2

1. RPYAR = 1. _____
   To turn aside; evade or dodge

2. TTSNBAE = 2. _____
   To thrive and prosper, especially at another's expense

3. SCLIOENEN = 3. _____
   Rude or impertinent behavior or speech

4. IIEECGDR = 4. _____
   The killing of a king

5. PNMHSY = 5. _____
   Female spirits who lived in forests, bodies of water, and other places outdoors

6. WONNER = 6. _____
   Widespread and high repute; fame

7. CREEBEXLA = 7. _____
   Utterly detestable; abominable; very bad

8. SNSBEASE = 8. _____
   Characteristic of or befitting an inferior person or thing

9. EOMLNS = 9. _____
   Causing serious thoughts or a grave mood

10. AORRLEBIT =10. _____
    Someone who releases people from captivity or bondage

11. AISPNUPTL =11. _____
    One who asks humbly and earnestly

12. EEMSUPR =12. _____
    To take for granted, assume, or suppose

13. RPAAUGSET =13. _____
    The activity or business of pasturing livestock

14. ELAICIOTMDN =14. _____
    The utterance of a curse

Oedipus Vocabulary Juggle Letters 2 Answer Key

1. RPYAR = 1. PARRY
   To turn aside; evade or dodge

2. TTSNBAE = 2. BATTENS
   To thrive and prosper, especially at another's expense

3. SCLIOENEN = 3. INSOLENCE
   Rude or impertinent behavior or speech

4. IIEECGDR = 4. REGICIDE
   The killing of a king

5. PNMHSY = 5. NYMPHS
   Female spirits who lived in forests, bodies of water, and other places outdoors

6. WONNER = 6. RENOWN
   Widespread and high repute; fame

7. CREEBEXLA = 7. EXECRABLE
   Utterly detestable; abominable; very bad

8. SNSBEASE = 8. BASENESS
   Characteristic of or befitting an inferior person or thing

9. EOMLNS = 9. SOLEMN
   Causing serious thoughts or a grave mood

10. AORRLEBIT = 10. LIBERATOR
    Someone who releases people from captivity or bondage

11. AISPNUPTL = 11. SUPPLIANT
    One who asks humbly and earnestly

12. EEMSUPR = 12. PRESUME
    To take for granted, assume, or suppose

13. RPAAUGSET = 13. PASTURAGE
    The activity or business of pasturing livestock

14. ELAICIOTMDN = 14. MALEDICTION
    The utterance of a curse

www.ingramcontent.com/pod-product-compliance
Lightning Source LLC
LaVergne TN
LVHW081534060526
838200LV00048B/2084